P R A I S E F O R

Strictly Sundays

Dear Mom really hit the jackpot, for son Joseph proved to be an expert cook and a big help in the kitchen, where a deep bond enabled him to collect many of Mom's and Grandma's recipes. But we all hit the big time with Joe's skills in the kitchen. For years, thanks to him, fine food flavors have drifted over the Fitzpatrick family's Sunday traditions. Joe's great cooking brought the kids and then the grandchildren and sometimes even a friend or two. I'm thrilled that Joseph now shares with the public the successes that I and so many other folks have urged him to do.

— **Leslie Fitzpatrick**

Our father's cooking never ceases to amaze. He has introduced us to flavors and dishes from all over the world, and the best part, we get to "go out" in the comfort of our own home.

— **Angela and Zackary Adams**

Joe's meals put food at the center of family get-togethers, and his special touch surrounds all with love, connection, and sharing. His creative recipes keep family members gathering!

— **Nancy Bush**

As a longtime friend of Joe's, I can tell you firsthand how he has evolved into a master cook. The secret to his success is to experiment and, more important, have fun with it. Eating at Joe's is pure entertainment, and his dishes are simply delicious and over the top.

— Jim and Ashley Shasky

Eclectic yet exotic in taste. Sensual yet cerebral in concept. Dining with him is such a delicious experience. Joe? Clever, creative, a true culinary inventor.

— Leslie Cornish

I look forward to Memorial Day weekend for one reason only... Joe's cooking. From the wonderful aroma that envelopes you when you first walk in the door... to that first succulent bite...to the last delicious lick of your fingers... you are in heaven.

— Barbara Sloate

I used the amazing spicy shrimp appetizer disk as a main course. I served it over rice and French bread. It is a meal that the whole family loved. Hat's off to the Sunday chef!

—The Hawkins Family

STRICTLY

Sundays

Written by

JOE FITZPATRICK

The Blue Collar Gourmet

BOOK PUBLISHERS NETWORK

Book Publishers Network
P.O. Box 2256
Bothell, WA 98041
425-483-3040
www.bookpublishersnetwork.com

10 9 8 7 6 5 4 3 2 1

Printed in the United States of America

LCCN: 2009907833
ISBN10: 1-935359-19-3
ISBN13: 978-1-935359-19-7

Editor: Julie Scandora
Indexer: Carolyn Acheson
Book Design: Laura Zugzda

*A portion of the proceeds of this book will be donated
to the John L. Scott Foundation that benefits
Children's Hospital in Seattle Washington.*

Dedication

I dedicate this book in loving memory of my mother, Doris. From a tender age, I learned from her that cooking can be fun and that a male *(in the 1960s)* should not be afraid to cook.

One night we were eating a special occasion meal in the dining room, and she asked me, all of ten years old, to put more dinner rolls in the oven. Obediently, I took the plastic bag of rolls, placed them on a cookie sheet, and put them in a 350° oven. About ten minutes later, a horrible smell emerged from the kitchen. The plastic bag had melted over all the rolls and was bubbling on the cookie sheet. I felt terrible, and my mom just said it was ok. She never scolded me for any of my bone-headed mistakes in the kitchen.

She taught me enough about cooking that when I was a bachelor living with the guys, I was usually the designated cook. To this day, I love cooking for my family on weekends. For that I will be eternally grateful.

Thanks, Mom!

Acknowledgements

I first thank my wife, Vickie, for appreciating the successes and tolerating the failures in making this book. I thank my children Angela, Kurtis, and Devin for not being afraid to try anything. Our Sundays have expanded to include Zac, William, Samantha, and my father, Les, who all enjoy and are brutally honest in the opinions of my dishes.

I also thank my culinary friends that have shared their recipes and appreciated mine. John and Sue Nagel, Leslie Cornish, Jeff and Lisa Johnson, Carl Gardner, Debbie Miles, Judy Gratton, Wynona Philpot, Rory's of Edmonds, cousin Gus Fitzpatrick, Uncle Ed, Paige Hall, and Jim and Ashley Shasky.

I thank my publisher Sheryn Hara of Book Publishers Network and all the talented people surrounding her.

I thank my photographer Steve Potter who took on this challenge with vigor and positive excitement. He really was a pleasure to work with.

I thank Richard Bush with Richard Bush Photography for taking a great picture of me on the back of this book.

And last but not least, thank you for purchasing my book. I hope it will be your "go to" resource for special eating occasions from now on.

TABLE OF *Contents*

My Story

Ever since I was a little boy, I enjoyed helping my mother cook in the kitchen. She made preparing food fun, and I learned a lot. Of course, that was in the 1960s when the only cook on television was Julia Child. There were no fancy spices or sauces used in our house, and all the meals were pretty basic. I have evolved since then.

No, I do not own a restaurant as do most credible cookbook authors. I just love to cook. My answer to the nay-sayers is, Why turn something you love to do into a job?

I owned a business in the 1980s and spent little time at home. My wife and I would make it a point to go out to dinner every Saturday night to spend some time with each other. When the business went away, so did the money for dinners out. But I still liked good food. I subscribed to *Bon Appetite* magazine and started to make unique intimate dinners for the two of us on Saturday nights.

Then our children got older, saw what we were having for our Saturday night gourmet dinner, and asked why they didn't get special meals too. So I started to explore and create both new and traditional dinners for them on Sunday nights. When the kids had jobs, I made a rule that Sunday was for faith and family, no exceptions. They almost never missed one of my Sunday dinners.

When my daughter Angela asked for my Caesar salad recipe, I said, *"I just do it and have never written it down."* So when I wrote it and gave it to her, she said, *"Why don't you write a cookbook dedicated to Sunday dinners?"* I thought it was a great idea and set out to craft a cookbook so an average person can be a hero on Sundays and holidays.

I have included old-fashioned dishes, now called comfort food, I loved as a youth and have also added contemporary, innovative recipes.

My hope is that you enjoy all of my dinners and share them with loved ones on those special occasions, like SUNDAYS!

— *Joe Fitzpatrick*

Appetizers

SPICY SHRIMP

The Shrimp
1 teaspoon paprika
1 teaspoon black pepper
1 teaspoon garlic powder
1 teaspoon onion powder
1 teaspoon Old Bay seasoning
1 teaspoon dried oregano
½ teaspoon cayenne pepper
1 teaspoon dried thyme
2 teaspoons lemon zest
30 uncooked shrimp or prawns, peeled and deveined

Combine all the ingredients and add the shrimp to coat.
Cover and chill 2-4 hours.

The Sauce
½ cup unsalted butter *(1 stick)*
3 tablespoons Worcestershire sauce
Juice of 1 large lemon
2 tablespoons chopped garlic
1 tablespoon chopped anchovies
2 teaspoons Dijon mustard
3 dashes Tabasco

Melt half of the butter and add the Worcestershire, lemon
juice, garlic, and anchovies. Sauté for 3 minutes until the
garlic is tender but not brown. Add the shrimp and the
remaining butter and sauté until the shrimp are a pretty
pink, stirring constantly.

Place in a bowl and dig in. Get some French bread for that
sauce!

SMOKED FISH WITH HERBED CREAM CHEESE ON ENDIVE

You can use any fish with this appetizer as long as it's smoked.

1 8-ounce package cream cheese, room temperature
½ cup fresh dill chopped
¼ cup minced red onion
1 teaspoon lemon zest
2 tablespoons capers
4 heads of Belgian endive
8-10 ounces smoked salmon or trout
3 tablespoons chopped chives

Mix the first 5 ingredients in a bowl. If made ahead, cover and chill; bring to room temperature when ready.

Separate endive leaves, spoon the herbed cream cheese on the leaves, top with a one-inch piece of fish and sprinkle with chives. Serve on a large platter.

MONICA'S GUACAMOLE

I had this at a company party and begged Monica for this recipe for my book. It is the best I have ever had.

4-5 Haas avocadoes, diced
2 Roma tomatoes, seeded and finely diced
1 cucumber, seeded and finely diced
6 green onions, chopped
4 Serrano peppers, diced
3 garlic cloves, minced
¾ cup chopped cilantro
1 tablespoon salt
½ tablespoon pepper
Juice of 1½ limes

Combine all ingredients in a large bowl, leaving one of the pits of the avocadoes in the mixture, and chill two hours.

Sometimes having an assortment of appetizers for dinner can be fun. Especially on Oscar night. Here are some of my favorites.

MUSTARD SEED PANCAKES WITH SMOKED SALMON AND CAVIAR

1¼ cups whole milk
2 tablespoons lemon juice
1 egg
3 tablespoons Dijon mustard
2 tablespoons mustard seeds
2 teaspoons creamy horseradish
1 cup Bisquick
3 tablespoons melted butter
3 tablespoons chopped fresh dill

Combine first 6 ingredients in a bowl and slowly mix in the Bisquick. Stir in the melted butter and dill. Cover and let it stand at room temperature for 1 hour.

Heat a skillet over medium heat. Melt butter or spray the skillet with cooking oil. Drop a tablespoon worth of batter in the skillet to make about a 2-inch pancake. Cook until golden on bottom and bubbling on top, about 3 minutes; turn and cook until golden. Place on a cookie sheet in a 200° oven to keep warm.

Serve the pancakes with:
Smoked salmon
Sour cream
Chopped red onion
Chopped dill
Caviar (You can find inexpensive but very good caviar in the canned fish section of most grocery stores.)
Capers

CRAB CAKES WITH DIPPING SAUCE

The problem restaurants typically have with crab cakes is they drown out the flavor of the crab with too many fillers and spices. This recipe is delicately good, respecting the crab flavor.

The Crab Cakes

4 cups breadcrumbs (make your own with crustless French bread in a processor or use store-bought)
12 ounces Dungeness crab meat (or any kind, but Dungeness is preferred)
2 tablespoons fresh chopped dill
$\frac{1}{2}$ cup finely chopped red onion
2 tablespoons capers
3 tablespoons mayonnaise
1 teaspoon lemon juice
1 teaspoon Dijon mustard
1 egg, beaten
1$\frac{1}{2}$ teaspoon Old Bay seasoning
2 tablespoons butter
2 tablespoons olive oil

Mix 2 cups breadcrumbs, crab meat, dill, onions, capers, mayonnaise, lemon juice, Dijon, egg, and Old Bay seasoning in a large bowl until well mixed. Make patties $\frac{1}{2}$-inch thick and coat them on both sides with the remaining breadcrumbs. Place on a cookie sheet and refrigerate 1-3 hours.

Melt butter and oil in a large skillet over medium heat. Sauté patties until golden brown, about three minutes per side.

Serve hot with dipping sauce.

Dipping Sauce
Easy and delicious.

½ **cup mayonnaise**
½ **cup sour cream**
1 **tablespoon Dijon mustard**
1 **tablespoon horseradish from a jar**
1 **tablespoon hot paprika**

Mix all ingredients together and spoon on top of the cakes,
or serve off to the side and dip.

PORTUGUESE MEATBALLS W/SPICY SAUCE

These are a great appetizer, or double the sauce and serve over pasta for a main course.

The Meatballs

1½ pounds ground veal
2 teaspoons salt
½ teaspoon crushed red pepper
1 tablespoon black pepper
1 tablespoon paprika
2 tablespoons chopped fresh cilantro
2 tablespoons chopped fresh flat-leaf parsley
3 garlic cloves, minced
½ cup yellow onion, minced or processed
1 tablespoon tomato paste
2 tablespoons buttermilk
4 large eggs
¾ cup breadcrumbs or Panko, separated
½ cup flour
5 teaspoons Creole spice *(store-bought)*
Canola oil for frying

Combine the veal, salt, red pepper, black pepper, paprika, cilantro, parsley, garlic, onion, tomato paste, buttermilk, 1 egg, and ¼ cup breadcrumbs in a large bowl and mix until well blended. Form meatballs with about 2 tablespoons of the mixture; they should be about the size of a golf ball.

Combine the flour and 1 teaspoon of the Creole spice in a separate bowl.

Beat the remaining 3 eggs in another bowl with 3 tablespoons cold water and 3 teaspoons Creole spice.

Combine the remaining ½ cup breadcrumbs and last teaspoon Creole spice in a third bowl.

Dip each ball into the flour first, the egg wash next, and then the breadcrumbs. Flatten them slightly to form a fat patty. Place on a wax-paper covered cookie sheet. Cover and refrigerate for 1-3 hours or overnight.

In a large sauté pan, add enough oil to come ½ inch up the side. Heat the oil to about 350°. Fry the meat pies in the oil in batches until they become a deep golden brown and are cooked through, about 3-4 minutes on each side. Cut one in half to be sure they are thoroughly cooked and adjust your timing accordingly. Drain on paper towels.

The Spicy Sauce

2 tablespoons olive oil
1 cup chopped onion
4 garlic cloves, minced
1 teaspoon crushed red pepper
2-3 anchovy fillets, minced
½ cup chopped kalamata olives
1 tablespoon tomato paste
1 28-ounce can crushed tomatoes
½ cup low-sodium chicken stock
2 tablespoons chopped parsley
2 tablespoons chopped cilantro
1 teaspoon dried thyme

In a saucepan, add the oil and sauté the onions and garlic until they are opaque, about 4-5 minutes. Add the red pepper, anchovies, and olives. Combine and cook 2 minutes. Add the tomato paste, crushed tomatoes, and chicken stock. Simmer for 30 minutes uncovered and stir occasionally. Serve over the meatballs.

BUFFALO WINGS

The Wings
20 chicken wings
2 cups flour
2 tablespoons garlic powder
1 tablespoon chili powder
1 teaspoon Ancho powder
4 cups peanut oil

Pat dry the wings and cut off the end nub at the joint. Mix flour and powders together in a pie plate. Heat the peanut oil in a deep fryer to 350.° Dredge the wings in the flour and deep fry in batches for 10-12 minutes. Remove and put them on paper towels.

The Sauce
1 7-ounce ancho chilies in adobe sauce, mashed or pureed in a processor
2 tablespoons Dijon mustard
2 tablespoons red wine vinegar
2 tablespoons honey
½ cup melted butter (1 stick)
1 tablespoon paprika
1 24-ounce bottle Frank's Red Hot

Combine all ingredients in a medium bowl.

Place the wings in a large baking dish, pour the sauce over the wings, cover, and bake in a 300° oven for 30 minutes.

Serve with a cup of blue cheese dressing, sliced celery, and LOTS of napkins.

Main Dishes

Barbeque

Not all meat is the same in barbecuing. Nor are all barbecues the same. I like to use a charcoal barbecue with a lid instead of gas because charcoal gives the meat a better flavor.

There are two methods of charcoal barbecuing, direct heat and indirect heat. For direct heat, you spread the coals after they are lit evenly across the bottom of the barbecue. Use this method when grilling steaks, chops, chicken, and vegetables.

For indirect heat, pile the coals away from the middle of the grill, usually two piles opposite each other. Use this method for roasting foul and roasts. When roasting with the indirect method, place a drip pan filled with hot water, beer, wine, or broth under the meat. This will insure your entrée will be moist and delicious when done.

Tips

Allow about 30 minutes for the coals to burn long enough to produce sufficient heat for cooking. The coals should have a slight coating of ash with no black showing.

When using a liquid starter, soak coals for 3 to 5 minutes before lighting.

Always use tongs when turning the meat. Premature piercing will dry the meat out. If you need to use a meat thermometer to check the temperature, try to wait until you are reasonably sure the meat is already done.

For a smokier flavor, soak wood chips in water for 30 minutes and throw a handful on top of the coals. The more wood used, the stronger the smoke flavor in the meat, so don't overdo it.

Sauce

My wife went to Kansas City some years ago and went to a famous barbecue restaurant and brought me home a jug of sauce and a rack of ribs. The sauce needed some taming with a store-bought sauce mixed in, and I have been looking for that flavor ever since.

I found it! In my opinion if someone has accomplished the true flavor of anything you're looking for why not use it? The Generals Spicy Bar-B-Que Sauce is the best sauce you can make or buy. It is distributed by Porter Foods, Inc., 19249 84th Avenue South in Kent, WA 98032 or www.thegeneralsBBQ.com.

I buy it by the gallon for about twenty dollars and add two chopped yellow or sweet onions and two 28-ounce cans of chopped tomatoes. I slather my victim of meat in it and bake in the oven at 275° for an hour or two after barbequing or smoking the meat.

HOMEMADE SPICY BAR-B-QUE SAUCE

This sauce is a good one for those people who don't believe in store-bought. I like to make a big batch to either drown the meat or chicken in or freeze in small containers to use at a later time.

2 cups chopped yellow onion
6-8 garlic cloves, chopped
3 large red peppers
2 tablespoon olive oil
1 64-ounce bottle of ketchup
1 46-ounce can of V-8 juice
1 cup brown sugar
½ cup Worcestershire sauce
½ cup cider vinegar
1 12-ounce beer
1 28-ounce can chopped tomatoes
1 tablespoon celery seed
2 tablespoons hot paprika
1 tablespoon crushed red pepper
2 tablespoons chili powder
1 tablespoon black pepper
2 tablespoons dried marjoram
2 tablespoons dried English hot mustard
1 cup orange juice

Chop the onion and garlic and set aside. Puree the red pepper in a food processor until smooth. Heat the oil in a large pot and sauté the onions and garlic for about 3 minutes. Add the pureed red pepper and simmer about 10 minutes. Add all the rest of the ingredients accept the orange juice. Simmer on low heat for 2-3 hours, partially covered and don't worry if it does not meet expectations yet. Let it finish blending together.

Add the orange juice about 15 minutes before introducing your meat to the sauce.

Place the meat in a large roasting pan, pour the sauce over, and place in a 300° oven for 45-60 minutes.

E N J O Y !

TRADITIONAL BARBECUE SAUCE

1 cup chopped yellow onion
2 garlic cloves, chopped
1 tablespoon olive oil
Salt
Pepper
1 cup dark molasses
1 28-ounce bottle of ketchup
¼ cup red wine vinegar
¼ cup bourbon
1 teaspoon paprika
1 tablespoon dry English mustard
1 tablespoon chili powder
1 teaspoon celery seed
1 teaspoon marjoram
Pinch of red pepper flakes

In a medium saucepan, sauté the onion and garlic in the olive oil until tender but not brown. Add the next 12 ingredients and simmer 1 hour. Can be kept in the refrigerator for 1 week or frozen 6 months.

RORY'S OF EDMONDS, WASHINGTON, BARBECUE SAUCE

I normally will not eat ribs in a restaurant because they can't compare to mine and I am usually disappointed. Rory's, just east of the ferry docks in Edmonds, Washington, is the exception. Their tasty ribs fall off the bone, and the sauce is fantastic! They were kind enough to share their recipe with me. I have cut the portions in half, and it still makes a lot.

½ **pound butter**
1 **cup bourbon** *(Jack Daniels)*
1 **cup dark brown sugar**
1 **cup honey**
1 **cup red wine vinegar**
1 **cup Worcestershire sauce**
1 **cup dark molasses**
½ **small bottle hot sauce** *(Tabasco)*
½ **tablespoon cayenne pepper**
1 **tablespoon chopped garlic**
1 **lemon, juiced**
1 **tablespoon black pepper**
1 **gallon Cattleman's BBQ Sauce**

Combine all the ingredients in a large pot and simmer for at least 1 hour.

STEAK MARINADE

Simple but delicious marinade.

3 cups soy sauce
½ cup red wine vinegar
1 cup white wine

Combine all ingredients. Best if marinated overnight.
No steak sauce for these!

BASIC BARBECUE RUB

I find that most commercial rubs contain too much salt.
However, the best seasoning on the market, in my opinion,
is Grill Mates Montreal Steak by McCormick.

If you want to play around with some rubs of your own here
is one of the basics.

2 tablespoons celery seed
1 tablespoon paprika
1 tablespoon chili powder
1 tablespoon garlic powder
1 tablespoon onion powder
2 tablespoons marjoram
1 tablespoon salt
1 tablespoon brown sugar
1 tablespoon dry mustard
1 tablespoon black pepper

In a plastic container with a tight fitting lid combine all
ingredients.

And if you want to bring some heat, add 1 tablespoon
cayenne pepper.

UNCLE ED'S CHICKEN MOP

½ pound butter (one stick)
I cup water
I tablespoon flour
I tablespoon A-I Steak Sauce
½ teaspoon Tabasco sauce
I tablespoon brown sugar
I teaspoon kosher salt
Pinch of cayenne pepper
2 teaspoons Worcestershire sauce
½ cup orange juice

Combine all ingredients in a saucepan and bring to a boil.
Apply to chicken every 5 minutes in the last 20 minutes of
cooking.

COUSIN GUS' COWBOY STEAK RUB

I tablespoon kosher salt
I teaspoon smoked paprika
I teaspoon granulated garlic
I teaspoon black pepper
I teaspoon dried ground thyme
I teaspoon fine ground coffee

Combine all ingredients and rub on your rib eye steaks
about an hour before cooking.

BEEF AND PORK POT ROAST WITH CARAMELIZED ONION GRAVY

This is a dinner first made by my mother, as far as I know. The pork and beef mixture make an excellent gravy alone, but the caramelized onion idea came from another chicken dish I saw on a cooking show.

The Base
4 tablespoons unsalted butter
2 medium yellow onions, chopped *(about 4 cups)*
Salt
Pepper
2 packages beefy onion soup mix
2 14.5-ounce cans chicken broth
3 cups red wine
2 cups water

In a large frying pan, melt the butter, add the onions, and sauté until golden brown, stirring frequently. Remove from the heat and put the onions in a large roaster. Mix in the salt and pepper to taste, onion soup mix, chicken broth, wine, and water with the onions and stir well to blend together.

The Roasts
1 3½-pound beef pot roast
1 3½-pound pork butt roast
4 tablespoons unsalted butter
2 tablespoons olive oil
6 tablespoons flour
Salt
Pepper

Heat the oil and butter in a large frying pan over medium heat. Salt and pepper the flour to your liking. Dredge the roasts in the flour and brown them in the butter and oil. Remove from the pan and place the roasts in the roasting pan.

Cook in a 350° oven for about 3 hours or until the meat is falling apart.

The Veggies
4 russet potatoes, peeled and cut into quarters
2-3 pounds boiler onions, peeled
4-5 carrots, peeled and cut into large chunks

Add the veggies to the roasts about 1 hour and 15 minutes before they are done.

The Gravy
3 tablespoons cornstarch
¾ cup cold water
Salt
Pepper

Pour the juices from the roasts into a large saucepan or deep skillet. Bring to a rolling boil, stirring constantly. Whisk the cornstarch into the cold water until the cornstarch completely dissolves. SLOWLY pour the cornstarch mixture into the sauce, stirring constantly until it thickens. It will take a minute or two before the cornstarch takes effect, so have patience.

Repeat if necessary. When you have the right consistency add salt and pepper to taste.

BLOODY MARY STEAKS

This is a variation of a recipe by Susan Asanovic on Allrecipes.com, and it got rave reviews.

Serves 6-8

4-6 rib eye or Spencer steaks, 6-8 ounces each
Olive oil
Black pepper
1 tablespoon celery seed
2 cups Bloody Mary mix
2 tablespoons frozen orange juice concentrate
1 tablespoon Worcestershire Sauce
Hot sauce to taste *(prefer Tabasco)*
3 tablespoons unsalted butter
20 pitted green olives
3 garlic cloves, finely chopped
8-10 marinated spicy green beans, cut at an angle in thirds

One hour before grilling the steaks, take them out of the refrigerator, sprinkle with the celery seed and pepper on both sides, and allow them to come to room temperature.

In a saucepan, heat up the Bloody Mary mix, orange juice, Worcestershire, and hot sauce. Simmer for 15 minutes.

In a blender or food processor, combine the butter, olives, and garlic and process until well combined and smooth.

Barbecue the steaks over medium hot coals 4 minutes per side for medium-rare and let stand at least 10 minutes before slicing.

To serve, spoon the sauce on the bottom of a large platter. Slice the steaks into one-inch slices, and arrange on the platter. Put a dollop of olive butter on each steak and sprinkle the green beans over and around the steaks. Makes a great presentation.

Serve with Twice-baked Potatoes (page 120) and a green salad.

HERBED PRIME RIB ROAST

Cooking with so much salt can be frightening at first, but don't worry. I have done this recipe several times with great success. It is delicious and as tender as a mother's love.

It is very important that you use coarse kosher salt. NOT rock salt, table salt, or pickling salt. Leftovers make great French dip sandwiches, and save the bones for French onion soup. They can be used the next week or frozen for a later time.

The Herbs

1 cup grated onion
1 tablespoon garlic powder
1 tablespoon dried thyme
1 tablespoon dried basil
1 tablespoon dried rosemary, crushed with a mortar and pestle to
  powder-form
2 teaspoons pepper
Olive oil

Combine first 6 ingredients in a bowl and add enough olive oil to form a paste. Makes about ¼ to ½ cup.

The Meat

1 bone-in rib roast, preferably a 7–rib,
  about 15-17 pounds
2 boxes coarse kosher salt
2½ cups water

Pat the meat dry with paper towels and spread the herb mixture over the top and sides of the roast. Cover in plastic wrap and refrigerate overnight.

Line with foil a roasting pan large enough to hold the roast. Mix the water and salt in a bowl to form a thick paste. Pat the salt mixture to form a ½-inch-thick rectangle along the middle of the bottom of the pan. Place roast on the salt, insert a meat thermometer, and pat a ½-inch-thick layer of salt enclosing the entire roast to form a seal.

Place the roast in a 425° oven and roast 16 to 18 minutes per pound for rare (132°), 20 to 22 minutes per pound for medium (140°), or 25 to 30 minutes per pound for well done.

Remove the roast when the thermometer registers 5° below desired doneness. If using an instant-read thermometer, check the roast 10-15 minutes before it is supposed to be done, checking in 5-minute intervals. Let it stand for 10 minutes in the crust before carving.

To remove the crust you may need to use a hammer. Use a pastry brush to remove the remaining salt particles. Slice and serve.

Serve with any potatoes in this book, green bean casserole, or sautéed asparagus. If this is for a holiday, add a soup and a salad.

STEAK FILLETS

If you buy the 2-inch thick fillets, this is how you cook them.

Salt
Pepper
3 tablespoons oil *(preferably canola oil for the high temperature)*

Let the fillets rest at room temperature for an hour before cooking.

Season with salt and pepper.

Preheat oven to 400.° Pour oil in a fry pan *(I prefer a cast-iron pan)*. Heat oil on medium-high and sear the steaks on one side for 3 minutes. Remove from the heat and put the pan in oven for 10-12 minutes. Do not turn the steaks over, and you will have a slightly charred side and a perfectly medium-rare side.

JOHN'S STUFFED FLANK STEAK

John and I go way back, and his is definitely a full-flavored dish that the family will rave about.

The Marinade
1½ pounds flank steak
10 garlic cloves, chopped
½ medium onion, chopped
2 tablespoons Worcestershire sauce
1 bottle (750ml) dry white wine
½ cup red wine vinegar
2 tablespoons dried thyme
1 envelope beefy onion soup mix

Pound out the flank steak with a meat mallet to tenderize. Mix all other ingredients together in a 13 x 9 x 2-inch baking dish. Add steak, coating with the mixture, cover with plastic wrap, and refrigerate overnight.

The Assembly
24 fresh basil leaves
½ pound Swiss cheese, sliced
2 sweet Italian sausages

Take the flank steak out of the marinade and pat dry. Discard marinade. Lay the flank steak flat on a work surface and lay the basil leaves on it, overlapping each other and leaving a ½-inch border along the edges. Cover the basil leaves with the Swiss cheese slices. Place the sausages end-to-end lengthwise in the middle of the flank steak.

Carefully roll the flank steak to wrap the sausages in the middle, and tie with string about every 1½ inches.

Continued on page 30

John's Stuffed Flank Steak
Continued from page 28

The Sauce
2 tablespoons olive oil
2 tablespoons butter
I large onion, thinly sliced
8 garlic cloves, chopped
I cup red wine
½ cup beef stock
¼ cup red wine vinegar
2 bay leaves
4 tablespoons fresh basil, chopped

Preheat oven to 350°.

Heat the oil and butter in a large oven-proof frying pan with a lid on medium to medium-high heat to brown the meat on all sides but not hot enough to burn. Remove the meat and set aside.

Add the sliced onion and sauté in the pan until they are a golden brown. Add the garlic, wine, beef stock, vinegar, bay leaf, and basil and bring to a boil. Add the flank steak back to the pan, cover, place in oven, and bake I hour.

The Finale
Take the flank steak out and let rest for 15 minutes. Meanwhile bring the sauce to a hearty simmer and reduce with the lid off.

Slice the steak in 1-inch servings and discard the string. Arrange on a serving platter and pour the sauce over, discarding the bay leaves.

Serve with orzo and thinly sliced basil with a tablespoon of olive oil, and cooked asparagus sprinkled with lemon and ½ cup Parmesan cheese.

Try not to blush from all the praise you will receive.

CABBAGE ROLLS

Pictured on page 31

Growing up, we used to call this dish "pigs in the blanket" when my mom would make them. I have changed the original recipe a little, but the basics are the same.

The Sauce

3 10¾-ounce cans tomato soup
1 14½-ounce can crushed tomatoes
1 14-ounce can beef broth
2 packages dry onion soup mix
3 tablespoons Worcestershire sauce
2 cups chopped onion
½ bunch Italian parsley, chopped
1 small can tomato paste

Combine all ingredients in a large saucepan and simmer for 20 minutes.

The Guts

1 pound ground beef
2-3 bratwurst sausages, casings removed
1 cup chopped onion
2 tablespoons tomato paste
2 10¾-ounce cans tomato soup
2 packages dry onion soup mix
1 cup minute rice
1 egg
2 tablespoons Dijon mustard
½ bunch parsley, chopped

Mix all ingredients together in a bowl until well incorporated.

The Cabbage
2 heads green cabbage

Fill a large pot of water ¾ full and bring to a boil. Cut the center core out of the cabbage by angling a knife around the core and pull it out. No need to cut too deep. Place the cabbage in the boiling water for 3-5 minutes. Remove and run under cold water until it is cool enough to handle. Peel off the leaves one at a time, careful not to tear.

The Assembly
Preheat oven to 325°.

Take out your big roasting pan with a lid and pour just enough sauce to cover the bottom. Lay out a cabbage leaf on a working surface and place about ½ cup of meat mixture on the core side of the leaf. Roll over once, tuck the sides in, and roll again. Place seam side down in the pan on top of the sauce. Repeat until all the meat mixture is used up, or if any meat mixture is left over, mix it in with the sauce. Discard the rest of the cabbage. Pour the remaining sauce over the cabbage rolls, cover, and bake for 2 hours. Remove the lid for the last half hour. Remove from the oven and let stand with the lid on for 20-30 minutes.

Serve with baked potatoes or twice-baked potatoes. You can put the potatoes in the oven at the same time as the cabbage rolls, and when the cabbage rolls are resting, you can assemble the potatoes in time to serve everything together.

The Finale
Place a cabbage roll on the plate, take a large spoon and press down on the middle of the roll making a slight indentation. Spoon some sauce in the middle and serve with the potatoes.

LONDON BROIL

This meal comes together very well with my olive-tomato topping.

The Marinade
4 tablespoons chopped
4 tablespoons balsamic vinegar
4 tablespoons lemon juice
3 tablespoons Dijon mustard
1 ½ tablespoons Worcestershire sauce
1 tablespoon soy sauce
1 teaspoon dried oregano
1 teaspoon dried basil
1 teaspoon dried ground rosemary
½ teaspoon cayenne pepper
1 teaspoon paprika
2/3 cup olive oil
½ cup red wine
2 1 ½-pound London broil steaks

Combine all the ingredients in a large sealable plastic bag, squeeze all the air out, seal, and marinate in the refrigerator overnight.

Remove from the refrigerator 1 hour before grilling. Heat the coals on the barbecue to medium-hot and grill the meat 8 minutes per side for medium-rare. Remove from the grill and let stand for 15 minutes before slicing. Thinly slice against the grain and arrange on a platter with slices overlapping

The Topping

2 cups cherry tomatoes, halved
I cup Italian parsley, chopped
½ cup chopped green olives
½ cup chopped Kalamata olives
½ cup chopped fresh basil
¼ cup extra virgin olive oil
2 tablespoons sherry wine vinegar

Combine all the ingredients two hours ahead and let sit at room temperature. Spoon the mixture over the sliced meat and serve.

Serve with Tomato-broccoli Salad (page 91) and Mustard-lime Potatoes (page 122).

BRAISED SHORT RIBS

I have played around with this recipe and it is similar to osso bucco and a great flavored comfort dish. When my son took his first bite, he said, "WOW!" Mission accomplished.

The Meat
6 pounds beef short ribs
3 tablespoons olive oil
2 cups flour
I tablespoon salt
I tablespoon pepper

In a large frying pan, heat the oil on medium-high. Mix the flour, salt, and pepper in a large bowl. Dredge the meat in the seasoned flour and brown the meat on all sides in batches. Place in a large Dutch oven or roaster pan with a lid.

The Sauce
I 750ml bottle Cabernet Sauvignon
2 tablespoons Dijon mustard
Olive oil
2 medium onions, chopped
3 large carrots, chopped
3 celery stalks, chopped
6 garlic cloves, minced
I 28-ounce can crushed tomatoes
2 14-ounce cans chicken broth
2 bay leaves
I tablespoon ground cardamom
I tablespoon ground coriander
2 teaspoons orange zest

While the meat is browning, pour the wine in a medium saucepan and gently boil until it is reduced in half. Wisk in the mustard until blended.

After the meat is brown, remove it from the pan, and add a little oil to the pan. Add the onions, carrots, celery, and garlic and sauté about ten minutes or until the vegetables are tender. Add the wine, can of tomatoes, broth, and the rest of the spices. Bring to a simmer and let it make love for about 10 minutes. Pour the sauce over the meat and cover.

Bake in a 350° oven for 3 hours, covered for 2 hours and the last hour with the lid off. OR: Bake in a 250° oven for 5-6 hours; strain the sauce and boil down about 20 minutes.

The Finale
6 russet potatoes, pierced several times with a fork
1½ cups butter *(3 sticks)*

Bake the potatoes along with the pot in the oven until a fork slides into them easily, about 1 hour and 15 minutes. Cut the potatoes in half and scoop the pulp into a large saucepan or pot. Add the butter and mash the potatoes until smooth, adding a little milk if necessary.

Spoon some of the potatoes onto a plate, top with meat and sauce. Serve some sautéed spinach alongside and enjoy.

KOLBI MARINADE

This is a great marinade for chicken, beef short ribs, or
flank steak.

3 cups soy sauce
2 tablespoons sesame oil
2 tablespoons honey
½ cup rice vinegar
2 tablespoons minced garlic
2 tablespoons minced ginger
I teaspoon crushed red pepper flakes *(or more for a*
   bigger bite)
I cup water
8-10 green onions, chopped
Zest of I orange
Zest of I lemon

Combine all ingredients in a large plastic bag or glass baking
dish with the meat of choice and refrigerate at least 2 hours
or overnight. Best if the meat is grilled on the barbie.

PERFECT POT ROAST

The Meat

5-6 pounds beef chuck roast
2 cups white flour
Salt
Pepper
4 tablespoons oil

Season the flour in a plate with salt and pepper. Dredge the roast in the flour. Heat the oil in a large frying pan on medium-high heat. Brown the meat on both sides, about 5 minutes per side. Place the roast in a large covered roasting pan.

The Liquid

2 packages Lipton Beefy Onion Soup Mix
1 15-ounce can tomato sauce or 1 can V-8 juice
20 ounces low-salt chicken broth
1 cups red wine

Sprinkle the onion soup mix on top of the roast and add the next three ingredients to the pan.

Place in a preheated 200° oven for 8 hours OR 300° oven for 3½ hours.

12-16 boiler onions
4 russet potatoes
4 medium carrots

Bring a large saucepan of water to a boil and add the onions for 30 seconds. Pour the water out and fill with cold water to stop the cooking process. Cut the hairy end off the onion and squeeze the onion out, discarding the skin.

Peel the potatoes and cut into eighths. Peel and cut the carrots into 2-inch pieces. Add the vegetables to the roasting pan, increase the heat to 325°, and bake all for an additional 45 minutes.

The Finale
1 cup cold water
½ cup white flour or 3 tablespoons cornstarch
Salt
Pepper

Remove the roast and vegetables to a serving platter and cover with foil. Whisk the water and flour until smooth with no lumps. Pour the liquid into a large saucepan or deep frying pan and bring to a boil. Stirring constantly slowly pour the flour and water mixture, ¼ cup at a time, until you reach the desired thickness. Taste first, and add salt and pepper to taste.

No variations on this one, but you can combine all the leftovers in a soup pot, chop the meat, and add more beef broth to make a wonderful beef stew for later in the week.

BEEF BOURGUIGNON

You may see this recipe as a French version of beef stew and think, So what? This is the chocolate mousse of beef stews...VERY RICH and delicious!

½ **pound bacon, chopped**
3 pounds beef chuck roast, cut into bite-size pieces
6 tablespoons flour
Salt
Pepper
2 tablespoons unsalted butter
2 medium yellow onions, thinly sliced
4 garlic cloves, minced
½ **cup cognac**
1 750ml bottle good red wine
2 cups low-sodium beef broth
1 tablespoon tomato paste
1 tablespoon fresh thyme *(or 2 teaspoons dried)*
2 bay leaves
1 tablespoon kosher salt
20-30 pearl onions

Fry the chopped bacon in a large skillet until just golden brown. Remove the bacon to paper towels to drain but keep the bacon grease.

Place the beef in a plastic bag, salt and pepper generously, add flour, and shake until all the beef chunks are covered with flour. Place in the pan and brown the meat in the bacon grease. When brown, remove from pan and set aside.

To the same pan, melt the butter and add the onions.
Sauté until golden. Add the garlic about 1 minute before the onions are done. Add the cognac, red wine, beef broth, tomato paste, thyme, bay leaves, and salt. Bring to a boil while scraping up all the yum-yums from the bottom. Add the bacon and meat. Stir and cover. Simmer 4 hours, stirring occasionally.

Peel the pearl onions per the directions and add them to the pot. Simmer another 30 to 45 minutes.

For a thicker sauce, add 2 tablespoons cornstarch in ¾ cup cold water. Whisk until smooth and slowly add to the sauce while stirring. The sauce should thicken nicely after a minute or two.

Serve with buttered potatoes.

SMOKED BRISKET OF BEEF

1 5-pound brisket of beef
Traditional barbecue sauce *(page 17)*
¼ cup bourbon
Alder chips

Fire up the electric smoker or use the indirect method on the barbecue. Soak the alder chips in water for ½ hour before starting. Place brisket in the smoker or barbecue, adding about 2 cups of chips every hour, and smoke for 8 to 10 hours.

Remove the meat with tongs and place in an oven roaster with a lid. Pour the traditional barbecue sauce and bourbon over the meat and bake in a 275° oven for 2 hours. Remove from the oven and shred the meat with two forks.

Serve on hamburger buns with Cheddar cheese and sliced sweet onion. Accompany with a green salad and Jo-Jo Potatoes (page 123).

TENDERLOIN STEAKS WITH BRANDY CREAM SAUCE

Do these steaks two at a time. This is a wonderful dish.

2 tablespoons butter
2 8-ounce, 1½-inch thick beef tenderloins
2 tablespoons Dijon mustard
1 teaspoon Worcestershire sauce
½ cup brandy (*Napoleon is very good and inexpensive*)
½ cup heavy cream

In a large frying pan, melt the butter on medium-high heat. Add the steaks and cook about 4 minutes per side for medium–rare, turning only once. Add the mustard and Worcestershire and stir.

Remove from heat to open area and away from exhaust fan. Add brandy and light with a match. Careful here not to get burned. It will flame 3 to 4 feet!

When the flames subside, place the steaks on a platter and cover with foil. Add cream to the pan and boil 5 to 10 minutes until it is reduced to a velvety consistency.

Pour the sauce over the steaks and serve with baby red potatoes and baked asparagus.

CORNED BEEF AND CABBAGE

Look for a good corned beef from a specialty store or a local butcher instead of the big grocery chains. I like to make enough corned beef to have Ruben sandwiches later in the week.

The Beef
5-6 pounds corned beef (usually two packages)
1 14-ounce can chicken broth
Cold water

Place the corned beef with all the spices in a large Dutch oven and cover with cold water. Add the chicken broth. Bring to a boil on medium-high heat, cover, reduce heat, and simmer for 4 hours.

The Vegetables
4 russet potatoes, peeled and quartered
1 head green cabbage, sliced or cut into eighths with core removed
10-12 whole boiler or small yellow onions, peeled

Additional Suggestions
Parsnips, carrots, beets, rutabagas

The Finale
Remove the corned beef and let rest for 20 minutes. Add the vegetables and bring to a soft boil for about 20 minutes or until the potatoes are fork tender. If you use any of the additional suggestions, they may take longer to cook, so add them about 15-20 minutes before removing the meat.

Thinly slice the corned beef against the grain. Serve with hot horseradish and Dijon mustard on the side.

SWISS STEAK

Like Mom usta make!

2 pounds bottom round steak
1 cup flour
2-3 tablespoons canola oil for frying
1 cup white wine
2 yellow onions, sliced
1 28-ounce can chopped tomatoes
1 tablespoon Worcestershire sauce
1 14-ounce can low-salt beef broth
1 package dry onion soup mix
2 cups water

Buy the thin-cut bottom round. Or, if it's not available, you will need to pound out the regular cut too.

Dredge the meat in the flour and fry on medium heat in the canola oil until brown on both sides. Working in batches, place them in a large roasting pan with a lid.

Deglaze the pan with the wine, scraping all the yum-yums from the bottom. Add the onions, tomatoes, Worcestershire, beef broth, and onion soup mix. Stir until incorporated well and add to the roaster.

Bake at 300° with the lid on for about 3 hours.

Serve with creamy mashed potatoes.

SPAGHETTI SAUCE

4 tablespoons olive oil
1 pound pork butt bone
1 lamb shank
1 pound Italian sausage links
4-5 large red bell peppers
1 large yellow onion
8 garlic cloves
1 bunch Italian parsley
6 sprigs fresh thyme
4 tablespoons fresh basil
1 tablespoon dried basil
½ tablespoon dried sage
1 tablespoon dried oregano
2 teaspoons dried rosemary, crushed
2 28-ounce cans crushed tomatoes
1 6-ounce can tomato paste
1 cup white wine
2 14.5-ounce cans chicken broth
1 tablespoon sugar
2 bay leaves
2 teaspoons red pepper flakes
Salt to taste
Pepper to taste
8-10 Roma tomatoes

In a large saucepot, heat the olive oil and brown the pork
and lamb shank. Remove and set aside. Cut the Italian
sausage into thirds and brown in the same pot. Remove and
set aside with the other meats.

While the meat is browning, seed and coarsely chop the red
peppers, place in a food processor, and chop to almost a
puree. Place in a bowl and do the same with the onion and
garlic. Combine the red pepper, onion, and garlic in a bowl

along with the next 7 ingredients. When the meat is done, add the red pepper-onion mixture to the wonderful grease in the pot and sauté for 10 to 15 minutes. Add the next 9 ingredients and bring to a boil. Add the meat and juices to the pot and lower the heat. Cover the pot and simmer at least 3 hours, stirring occasionally.

About 45 minutes from serving time, boil the tomatoes for 1 minute, place in cold water, and peel the tomatoes. Add to the sauce and simmer 45 minutes to 1 hour.

Remove and discard the meats.

Bon Appitito!

SPAGHETTI BASIC EASY SAUCE

This is easy but good if you're in a hurry. You may never buy jarred sauce again.

2 28-ounce cans tomato sauce
2 28-ounce cans crushed tomatoes
4 28-ounce cans water
1 large can tomato paste
6-8 garlic cloves, minced
2 yellow onions, peeled and quartered
4 tablespoons Schilling brand Italian seasoning
Zest from ½ orange
6-8 Italian sausages (sweet or spicy)

Combine all the ingredients in a large saucepot over medium heat. Reduce heat and simmer for 1 hour or until the sausages are done.

LADY VI'S LASAGNA

When my wife, Vickie, and I were first married, we met a wonderful German couple with a thick accent, and they called us Joy and Vi. To this day, our close friends still call her Vi. She makes me lasagna about twice each year, and it is a favorite of mine.

The Beginning

1 pound ground beef
1 pound Italian sausage
1 large onion, chopped
2 tablespoons Italian seasoning

Mix the Italian seasoning with the meats and brown them in a frying pan while chopping up. Add the onion near the end of browning so it is opaque but not brown.

The Sauce

2 28-ounce cans tomato sauce
3 15-ounce cans tomato sauce
2 28-ounce cans diced tomatoes with their juice
1 12-ounce can tomato paste
2 3.8-ounce cans sliced black olives, drained
3 heaping tablespoons Italian seasoning
4 tablespoons fresh oregano

Add all except the oregano to the meat and simmer 2 hours. Cool and refrigerate overnight.

Slowly heat up and simmer another 1½ hours. Toward the last 30 minutes, add the oregano.

The Assembly

Lasagna noodles, uncooked
2 cups chopped fresh basil
2 cups chopped fresh spinach
4 cups Mozzarella cheese
I cup shredded Parmesan cheese

Preheat oven to 350°.

Assemble in a 15 by 10 by 2-inch glass baking dish.
First spoon some sauce covering the bottom of the dish.
Then add:

A layer of uncooked noodles
Sauce to cover
Sprinkling of basil, spinach, and cheeses
Another layer of uncooked noodles
Sauce to cover
Repeat in this order, ending with sauce and then cheese on
the top.

Cover with foil and bake 45 minutes. Uncover and bake 15-
20 minutes until the top is golden brown. Remove from the
oven and let it stand for 15 minutes before serving.

BON APPITITO!

CHICKEN CACCIATORE

My feeling about cacciatore is like meatloaf ... anything goes. Adding all kinds of ingredients together to see how they blend is surprisingly fun and delicious. This version is slow cooked just because slow lends itself to a well-balanced flavorful dish. Enjoy.

The Chicken

12 boneless chicken thighs
3 boneless chicken breasts, cut in half
6 lemons
12 garlic cloves, chopped
2 tablespoons dried Italian seasoning
½ bottle white wine

In a large glass baking dish, squeeze the juice from the lemons. Add garlic, Italian seasoning, and the wine. Mix well and then add the chicken. Marinate 8 hours or overnight.

The Sauce

2 cups chopped onion
9 garlic cloves, chopped
5 tablespoons olive oil, divided
Salt to taste
Pepper to taste
2 28-ounce cans chopped tomatoes
1 28-ounce can tomato sauce
1 cup white wine
1 14-ounce can chicken broth
5 anchovies, chopped
4-6 tablespoons fresh basil, chopped
4 tablespoons Italian parsley, chopped
3 bay leaves
2 large sprigs thyme
1 orange pepper, chopped

Optional other additions:
Green pepper, chopped
Artichoke hearts, quartered
Green beans
Zucchini, chopped
1 6-ounce jar green olives, drained
1 6-ounce jar black olives, drained
1 4-ounce jar capers, drained
2 cups chopped mushrooms (shiitakes are nice)
3/4 cups seasoned flour
3 tablespoons olive oil
About 2 ounces Parmesan cheese

Continued on page 54

Chicken Cacciatore

Continued from page 53

Sauté onion and garlic in 2 tablespoons olive oil on medium heat until opaque. Add salt and pepper to taste. Add next 10 ingredients (and/or any of the optional suggestions) and simmer 4-6 hours, covered.

Remove chicken from marinade and pat dry. Dredge chicken in flour and brown in a frying pan with the remaining 3 tablespoons oil about 3 minutes per side

Remove the bay leaves and sprigs of thyme from the sauce. Drain the olives and capers, rinse well under cold water, and add to the sauce. Place the browned chicken in a 15 by 10 by 2-inch glass baking dish and pour the sauce over. Bake at 350° for 90 minutes. Half an hour before it's done, take your potato peeler and shave the Parmesan on top.

The Finale

6 cloves garlic chopped
2 tablespoons olive oil
½ cup chopped Italian parsley
1 pound spaghetti noodles

Boil spaghetti noodles in salted water until al dente. Sauté chopped garlic in oil. When spaghetti is done, drain and add to the pan of garlic. Sprinkle with parsley and mix well.

To serve on individual plates, place spaghetti on the bottom and top with chicken and sauce, picking out some of the goodies of your choice.

Accompany with garlic bread, salad, and a nice glass of red wine.

LEMON-GARLIC CHICKEN

Great on the grill. But very good oven-baked also.

The Marinade

7 lemons
Zest of I lemon
I medium onion, chopped
8 garlic cloves, chopped
6 sprigs fresh thyme or I tablespoon dried
3 cups dry white wine
2 tablespoons Dijon mustard
I tablespoon Worcestershire sauce

Juice 6 lemons and slice I. Combine all the ingredients in a large bowl.

The Chicken

12 chicken thighs

Place the chicken and marinade in a plastic bag or in a 15 by 10 by 2-inch glass baking dish and marinate for at least 4 hours, preferably overnight, turning occasionally.

Remove from the marinade and discard marinade. Cook uncovered in the oven at 350° for 50-60 minutes. Barbecue (preferred) for about 40-45 minutes, turning every 5-10 minutes. Be sure to spray oil on the grill to prevent sticking.

Serve with Dijon pasta and asparagus.

1 3 to 5-pound roasting chicken
Spicy chicken rub or a Mexican spice rubs, such as chipotle.
1 cup sour cream
8 ounces mild green chilies
6 green onions, chopped
¾ cup chopped cilantro
3 ounces sliced black olives
1 cup shredded Parmesan cheese
1 teaspoon chili powder
1 tablespoon paprika
10 medium-size flour tortillas
2½ 19-ounce cans green enchilada sauce
3 cups grated sharp Cheddar cheese

Preheat oven to 400°.

Rub the chicken over and under the skin with the spice rub of your choice. Remove the giblets and salt the cavity. Place on a rack in a covered roasting pan and roast for 1 hour or until the chicken reaches at least 165° internal temperature. Remove from the oven and let it cool for 30-45 minutes.

Reduce oven temperature to 350°.

Discard the skin and shred the chicken in a large bowl. Mix in the sour cream, green chilies, green onion, cilantro, olives, Parmesan cheese, chili powder, and paprika. Pour enough enchilada sauce on the bottom of a 15 by 10-inch glass baking dish just to cover. Place about ¾ cup chicken mixture on the bottom third of a flour tortilla and roll, placing the enchilada seam side down in the baking dish. Repeat until done. Pour the rest of the enchilada sauce over the top, and cover the top with Cheddar cheese.

Cover the baking dish with foil and bake for about 45 minutes or until the cheese on top is melted and bubbly. Let it cool for 10 minutes before serving.

Accompany with refried beans topped with Parmesan cheese and sliced avocadoes. To kick the heat up a little, I recommend Mrs. Renfro's green salsa.

CHAMPION SMOKED CHICKEN

Chicken thighs
Wishbone Italian salad dressing
Chicken rub (store-bought)
Spray
1 part soy sauce to 2 parts apple juice *(e.g., 1/3 cup soy sauce plus 2/3 cup apple juice)* **in a spray bottle**
Wood chips *(prefer alder)*
Glaze
Equal parts of ketchup, honey, raspberry vinaigrette, with ¼ cup soy sauce

Marinate the chicken in the Italian dressing overnight.

Pat the chicken and apply rub over and under the skin.

If using charcoal use the indirect heat method, or use your smoker. Try to keep the temperature around 275° to 300°.

Place chicken on the grill, skin side up. After 30 minutes, spray with soy sauce/apple juice mixture; turn the chicken over and spray again. In another 30 minutes, turn the chicken and spray again.

After 1 hour, add about 1½ cups wood chips and apply the glaze and turn. Repeat the glaze every 15 minutes until done.

Total time should be 1½ hours at this temperature. If you have a 200° smoker, they may take longer.

FRENCH BLT—OH MY!

These sandwiches are a great summertime meal. Requested by the kids several times.

What You Need for 6 BLTs
1 cup basil, chopped
1 cup mayonnaise
1 pound thick-sliced bacon
12 slices French bread (toasting optional)
3 large tomatoes, sliced
3 avocadoes
½ cup shredded Parmesan
1 lime, juiced
Salt
Pepper
1 red onion, thinly sliced
6 leaves romaine lettuce

Mix the basil and mayonnaise together in a bowl and set aside.

Cut the bacon in half for evenly cooked meat. Fry the bacon in a frying pan and drain on paper towels.

Peel and mash the avocado in a bowl with a fork until smooth. Mix in the lime juice to preserve the color and the Parmesan cheese for flavor. Add salt and pepper to taste.

The Assembly
On one slice of the bread, spread the basil mayonnaise. On the other slice spread the avocado mixture. Add the bacon, tomato, onion, and lettuce. Cut in half and enjoy.

Serve with pasta, potato salad, or tomato salad with Southwest scalloped potatoes (page 114).

The Rub

2 1½-2-pound pork tenderloins
2 teaspoons paprika
I teaspoon chili powder
I teaspoon garlic powder
I teaspoon onion powder
2 teaspoons dried marjoram
I teaspoon salt
I teaspoon black pepper
½ teaspoon cayenne pepper
I teaspoon dried thyme

Place the tenderloins fat side down in a 13 by 9 by 2-inch glass baking dish. Mix all the spices in a separate bowl and, with your hands, evenly rub the spices all over the meat. Cover with plastic wrap and refrigerate overnight.

Remove from the refrigerator 1 hour before cooking.

Bake in a 350° oven for 45 to 60 minutes or until the internal temperature is 160°. OR fire up the barbecue 1 hour before cooking to have medium-heat coals and place the meat on the grill for 35 to 45 minutes covered, turning occasionally. Remove from the oven or grill and let stand for 15 minutes before slicing.

The Sauce

6 medium Bosc or Bartlett pears *(Peaches may also work well.)*
2 tablespoons butter
2 tablespoons olive oil
¼ cup shallots, chopped
2 cups chicken broth
1¼ cups tawny port wine
1½ tablespoons whole-grain Dijon mustard
1 tablespoon regular Dijon mustard
2 tablespoons green peppercorns, drained and crushed

Peel, core, and slice the pears into quarter pieces. Heat the butter and olive oil in a large frying pan on medium-high heat. Fry the pears on each side until golden brown. Remove from the pan and set aside.

In the same pan add the chopped shallots and sauté until soft but not brown. Add the rest of the ingredients and simmer 20-30 minutes for it to thicken slightly. Just before serving, add the pears to the sauce and let them heat up about 5 minutes.

The Finale

Slice the pork and arrange on a platter. Place a pear slice on each slice of pork; pour the sauce over and serve.

Accompaniments

Sauté 2 bags of fresh spinach and 6 cloves of garlic, chopped, in 2 tablespoons olive oil in a large frying pan until wilted but not dead.

Serve with Sausage-Dijon Potatoes (page 117).

PULLED PORK

The Rub

1 tablespoon paprika
1 tablespoon brown sugar
1 tablespoon garlic powder
1 tablespoon onion powder
1 ½ teaspoons salt
1 tablespoon dry mustard
1 teaspoon black pepper
½ teaspoon cayenne pepper
2 teaspoon thyme
1 6-pound pork shoulder or pork butt

Combine all the ingredients except the pork and rub into the roast. Cover and refrigerate overnight.

The Sauce

3 tablespoons olive oil
2 cups chopped yellow onions
2 bottles Cattleman's Original Barbecue sauce
¼ cup Dijon mustard
¼ cup red wine vinegar
¼ cup brown sugar
1 cup water
1 teaspoon crushed red pepper flakes

Sauté the onion in the olive oil until the onion is soft and opaque. Add the remaining ingredients.

Pour the sauce into your slow cooker. If you don't have one, you can use a soup pot on the stove top. Place the pork in the sauce and simmer on a low heat for 4-6 hours.

Take the roast out of the sauce (it should be falling apart) and place it on a cutting board. Let it stand for 10 minutes; then take 2 forks and shred the meat. Serve with the sauce on the side all by itself or on a bun.

Serve with a salad and baked beans.

OSSO BUCO

Pictured on page 65

Traditionally, osso buco is made with veal shanks, but we love lamb, and it works very well. The first time I had this dish was at a friend's house, and I couldn't believe the huge flavor it had without a lot of spices.

The Lamb

¾ cups flour

Salt

Pepper

6 lamb shanks or request from your butcher 3 shanks
   cut from the hind end (more meat)

½ cup unsalted butter (I stick)

3 tablespoons olive oil

Mix salt and pepper to taste in the flour and dredge the shanks. Brown the meat in the butter and olive oil using a large skillet on medium to medium-high heat. Remove shanks and set aside.

The Sauce

1½ cups white wine

2 cups finely chopped onion (about I large yellow
   onion)

2 cups finely chopped carrot (about 2 large)

2 cups finely chopped celery (about 6 medium stalks)

4-6 garlic cloves, chopped

I tablespoon orange zest

I tablespoon lemon zest

I cup loosely packed chopped fresh basil

I 28-ounce can chopped tomatoes

2 14-ounce cans chicken broth

I cup loosely packed chopped parsley

4 sprigs thyme

2 bay leaves
2 tablespoons pomegranate molasses (optional)
1 box orzo

Using the skillet from browning the meat, deglaze the pan
with the white wine, scraping and blending all the goodies
from the lamb. Add the onion, carrot, and celery. Sauté until
opaque, about 5-10 minutes. Add garlic and zests and sauté
another 10 minutes. Add next 6 ingredients and bring to a
simmer.

Place shanks in a large roasting pan with a lid, reserving
skillet for use later. Pour sauce over shanks, cover, and bake
in a 325° oven for 3 hours.

Remove shanks. Separate meat to a holding platter. Ladle
sauce to original large skillet, removing the bones, fat, bay
leaf, and thyme sprigs. Add pomegranate molasses and cook
the sauce on a high simmer for 15 minutes to reduce
slightly. Skim fat from the top of the sauce. Add the meat
back into the sauce to keep warm.

The Finale
Boil the orzo according to the box directions and drain.
Serve a large spoonful of orzo on your plate or bowl and
top with meat and sauce. Serve immediately.

Accompany with a loaf of hot, thick-crust French bread.
There are plenty of vegetables in the sauce, but a side salad
works, too.

CRAB AND SCALLOP LASAGNA

This dish seems a little over the top, but it is quite good.

3 tablespoons unsalted butter
1 yellow onion, finely chopped
8 garlic cloves, minced
5 tablespoons all-purpose flour
5 cups half-and-half
12 lasagna noodles, uncooked
1 pound crab meat
1 pound scallops, cut into quarters
2 cups mozzarella cheese
1 cup chopped red pepper
1 cup cilantro, chopped
1 cup flat-leaf parsley, chopped
1 cup grated Parmesan cheese

Preheat oven to 375°. Spray a 15 by 10 by 2-inch glass baking dish with cooking spray.

Melt the butter in a large skillet and cook the onion and garlic until the onion is soft, about 5 minutes. On medium-low heat, whisk in the flour and slowly add the half-and-half. Allow the sauce to thicken and come to a simmer.

Spoon enough sauce into the glass baking dish to cover the bottom. Place the uncooked lasagna noodles to cover the bottom. Sprinkle with half of the crab, scallops, mozzarella, red pepper, cilantro, and parsley. Ladle sauce on top to cover, add another layer of noodles, and the other half of the 6 ingredients. Sprinkle the Parmesan on top and bake uncovered 30-45 minutes until bubbly and the noodles are soft. Pierce with a fork to test for doneness. Allow to sit for 10 minutes before slicing.

Serve with a green salad and garlic bread.

VEAL SCALOPPINE MARSALA

2 pounds veal scaloppini
Salt
Pepper
2 cups white cornmeal
4 tablespoons herbs de Provence
Unsalted butter
Olive oil
2 pounds crimini mushrooms
½ cup dry Marsala wine
½ cup cream
I tablespoon Dijon mustard
I cup low-salt chicken broth
½ cup chopped Italian parsley

Salt and pepper the veal. Mix cornmeal and the herbs.
Dredge the veal in the cornmeal. Cook in 2 tablespoons
butter and I tablespoon oil, adding more as needed, until
browned on all sides. Remove and let the veal rest.

Add mushrooms to the pan and sauté until brown. Add
Marsala and deglaze. Add cream, Dijon, and chicken broth.
Simmer until reduced. Add parsley and serve over veal.

Accompaniments
Serve with pasta sautéed in butter and parsley or with
fettuccine Alfredo.

Accompany with broccoli sautéed in oil and garlic with
Asiago cheese.

LAMB STEW

Ask your butcher to chop up a leg of lamb for stew. You should end up with about 2 pounds.

The Marinade

2-3 pounds lamb meat trimmed of all fat and tallow, chopped into bite-size pieces.
1 cup flour
1 tablespoon lemon pepper
1 teaspoon dried thyme
1 teaspoon dried rosemary, powdered with a bowl and pestle
1 teaspoon garlic powder

Place the meat in a zip lock bag with the flour and shake to coat. Put the meat in a bowl and add the spices. Cover and refrigerate 1-3 hours or overnight.

The Meat

3 tablespoons olive oil
¾ cup white wine
2 carrots, chopped
3 stalks celery, chopped
1 large onion, chopped
1 large parsnip, chopped
4 garlic cloves, chopped

Drag out the big soup pot. Add the olive oil and heat on medium-high. Sauté the lamb until brown, remove the meat, and put it back in the bowl. Deglaze the pot with the wine and scrape up the brown yum yums that have stuck to the bottom. Add the veggies and sauté until the opaque in color but not brown.

The Sauce

2 tablespoons tomato paste
1 cup red wine
1 15-ounce can tomato sauce
32 ounces chicken broth
¾ cup chopped fresh cilantro
¾ cup chopped fresh Italian parsley
1 tablespoon orange zest
1 large orange, peeled and chopped

Put the meat back into the pot and add all of the sauce ingredients. Simmer uncovered on low for 2 hours.

Accompaniments

Serve with hot French bread. Cook some orzo pasta and put a scoop or two in the bottom of the bowl when serving.

MOM'S GOULASH

Comfort food made in the sixties before they called it comfort food. Basic and oh so good.

The Basics
1 pound thick-sliced bacon
1 pound hamburger
3 stalks of celery
½ sweet or yellow onion
2 large carrots
2 tablespoons butter

Cut the bacon into ½-inch sticks and fry in a large pan until brown. Remove to a plate with paper towels to drain. In the bacon grease, fry the hamburger leaving it in 1-inch chunks. Drain and discard the grease. Set both meats aside.

Mince the celery, onion, and carrots as small as possible to measure about 1 cup each. Melt the butter in the frying pan and sauté the vegetables until opaque. Place in a ovenproof pot with a lid.

The Rest of the Story
1 package onion soup mix
4 cans tomato soup
1 cup beef broth
2 cups tomato sauce
1 28-ounce can chopped tomatoes, drained
3 russet potatoes
20 boiler onions

Preheat oven to 350°.

Add the onion soup mix, tomato soup, beef broth, and chopped tomatoes to the pot of vegetables and simmer 20 minutes. Peel and chop the potatoes into bite-size chunks. Add the potatoes and the meats to the pot, cover, and bake 1-1½ hours until potatoes are tender.

While the meat cooks, peel the boiler onions by placing them in a pot of boiling water for 30 seconds. Remove them from the heat and submerge in cold water until cool. Cut the hairy end off the onion and squeeze the onion out of its skin. Add the onions to the goulash about 20-30 minutes before it's done.

Serve with some hot French bread or rolls and butter.

BUTTER POACHED LOBSTER

If you have ever boiled a live lobster only to end up with a tough and chewy fish, it is because it was boiled and not steeped. Follow these directions for a perfect lobster tail every time.

You will need two large pots. Put the lobsters in one and fill with enough cold water to cover them. Remove the lobsters and put them in the empty second pot. Bring the water to a boil, adding ½ cup white distilled vinegar for every 8 quarts of water. Pour the boiling water over the lobsters and let them steep for 2 minutes for 1½ pounds of lobster or 3 minutes for 2 pounds of lobster.

Use gloves to remove the hot lobster, hold the tail, and twist it off the body and set aside. Pull the claws off and return to the water for 5 minutes.

Hold each tail flat and gently pull the meat out the large opening of the shell. Lay the meat on its back, cut down the middle, and remove the vein running through the top of the meat.

Remove the claws from the water. Pull down on the pincer and push it aside to crack it. Use a hammer to crack the shell to remove the meat.

In a saucepan, prepare the butter. This preparation is commonly called beurre monté.

Emulsify from 4 tablespoons to 1 pound of unsalted butter with only one tablespoon of water: Bring the water to a boil in an appropriate sized saucepan, lower the heat to low and add the butter in chunks, whisking constantly until you have the amount of beurre monté to poach the lobsters.

Beurre monté should be maintained at 180° to 190° to assure it does not separate. Place the tails and claws in the beurre monté and gently poach for 5 to 6 minutes.

Remove from the butter sauce and serve immediately.

You can also cut the tails and claws into chunks and add to my Macaroni and Cheese recipe for an over-the-top dish.

CEVICHE TOSTADAS

I had a version of these tostadas in Mexico and fell in love with the flavor of the white fish and lime juice. The lime juice actually cooks the fish as it marinates. You will want to use a hearty fish like halibut because a thinner fish like cod or sole will turn to mush.

The Fish

2 pounds halibut, skinned
I pound shrimp, peeled and deveined
10-12 limes
5 Anaheim chilies

Place fish and cleaned shrimp in a glass baking dish. Squeeze the juice of limes on the fish until the fish is completely covered in lime juice. Marinate for 4-6 hours in the refrigerator. Longer than 6 hours may overcook the fish, making it tough.

Blacken the chilies on the barbecue or in the oven on broil. Place in a paper bag for 20 minutes. Remove from the bag, peel and remove seeds. Chop the peppers and set aside.

The Topping

4 jalapeño chilies
2 Habanero chilies
4 medium tomatoes
½ head green cabbage, thinly sliced like coleslaw
6 garlic cloves, chopped
I cup chopped cilantro
½ medium red onion, thinly sliced
8 radishes, chopped
2 limes, juiced
I ounce tequila

Continued on page 78

Continued from page 77

Chop the chilies in a processor, put in a small serving bowl, and set aside.

Seed the tomatoes: Cut in half and cut the whitish part of the main membrane. Take the back of a spoon and pop out the seeds. Then chop the tomatoes. Combine all the ingredients except the chilies in a salad-type bowl and refrigerate for 1 hour.

The Finale

12 medium ripe avocadoes
Salt to taste
1 lime
12 tostada size corn tortillas
1 cup vegetable oil
1 cup grated Parmesan cheese

Peel and mash the avocadoes with a fork in a glass bowl. Add the salt and the juice of the lime. Mix well, leaving no chunks.

Drain the lime juice from the fish and discard. Chop the fish into ½-inch chunks. Chop the roasted Anaheim chili and combine with the fish.

Take a tostada and a good scoop of the mashed avocado and spread evenly over the tostada shell. Next, add some fish and top with the cabbage salsa. Sprinkle the top with Parmesan cheese and serve.

I serve the chopped jalapeño mixture separately for different people's taste in heat.

Serve with a Spanish rice from the box or my Green Rice (page XX?). Also, heat up some refried beans from a can and top with Parmesan cheese.

CEDAR PLANK SALMON

You can find cedar planks at most grocery or even lumber stores.

3 ½ pounds salmon (2 fillets)
Salt
Pepper
2 tablespoons fresh thyme
4 tablespoons fresh dill
2 tablespoons fresh basil
6 garlic cloves
2 tablespoons brown sugar
3 tablespoons fresh chives
I lemon, juiced
2 tablespoons olive oil
2 lemons, thinly sliced
2 cedar planks

Place the salmon fillets in a large glass baking dish, skin-side down. Salt and pepper the meat. Combine the next 8 ingredients in a food processor and process, making a slightly runny marinade. Spoon the marinade over the salmon. Place the sliced lemons on top. Cover with plastic wrap and refrigerate 2-6 hours.

Soak the cedar planks in water for 2-4 hours. Weigh them down with a heavy clean object so they don't float.

Fire up the barbecue I hour before cooking to ensure medium-hot coals. Place the salmon skin-side down on the cedar planks and place on the barbecue grill. Cover and cook about 8 minutes per pound or, in this case, 20-30 minutes.

DO NOT leave unattended in case of fire. If this occurs, have a squirt bottle of water on hand to douse the flames.

Remove the salmon from the planks when done or the fish will keep cooking. Discard the planks.

Serve with a tomato-avocado salad, Mustard Mashed Potatoes (page 119), or Roasted Pepper Rice (page 128).

CIOPPINO

2 tablespoons olive oil
4 red peppers, chopped
1 large yellow onion, chopped
8 garlic cloves, chopped
½ cup Italian parsley, chopped
1 tablespoon dried thyme (or ¼ cup fresh, chopped)
2 tablespoons dried basil (or ½ cup fresh, chopped)
½ tablespoon dried sage (or 2 tablespoons fresh, chopped)
2 teaspoons dried oregano (or 1 tablespoon fresh, chopped)
1 teaspoon dried rosemary (or 2 teaspoons fresh, chopped)

In a large soup pot, heat the oil and sauté all ingredients until soft. Add:

2 28-ounce cans chopped tomatoes
1 small can tomato paste
1 cup white wine
2 cups chicken broth
1 tablespoon sugar
2 bay leaves
1 teaspoon red pepper flakes
Salt to taste
Pepper to taste

Simmer for three hours on a low heat, partially covered and stirring occasionally.

With the sauce at a strong simmer add:

Mussels
Small clams

After 2 minutes, add:

Crab meat
Shrimp
**Any type of white fish: sea bass, cod, red snapper, or
   halibut.**

Cook until the fish is cooked, about 5-10 minutes.

Serve in bowls with hot French bread and a small salad on
the side.

FISH, CHIPS, AND TARTAR SAUCE

You will need a deep fryer with a basket for the chips and fish.

Tartar Sauce
1 cup mayonnaise
½ cup sour cream
½ cup chopped green onion
½ cup chopped dill pickle
2 tablespoons drained capers
1 teaspoon Old Bay seasoning
1 teaspoon garlic powder
1 tablespoon lemon juice

Mix all ingredients together and refrigerate 1-2 hours.

The Chips
4 russet potatoes
4 cups peanut oil

Peel and cut potatoes into ½-inch slices the length of the potato. Soak in cold water at least 1 hour. Towel-dry the potatoes.

Pour the oil in the fryer, about halfway. You don't want to overfill! Heat the oil to 325°. Place a large handful of potatoes in the basket and slowly submerge into the oil. Cook for 4 minutes, remove and drain on paper towels. Let them cool for 25 minutes.

Increase the temperature of the oil to 350° and return the partially cooked potatoes to the oil and cook until golden, about 5-6 minutes. Keep warm on a paper-lined cookie sheet in the upper part of a 250° oven.

1 cup flour
1 tablespoon Old Bay seasoning

Mix together in a pie plate.

1 ½ cups flour
1 tablespoon Old Bay seasoning
12 ounces beer, preferably amber ale
2-4 pounds cod fillets or fish of your choice, cut into 2-inch strips

Heat oil in the fryer to 375°.

In a glass baking dish, whisk together flour, seasoning, and beer. Pat dry 4-5 pieces of fish and first dredge in the dry flour then coat with the batter and carefully drop into oil. Cook about 5 minutes or until golden brown. Remove and place on a paper-lined cookie sheet and keep warm in the bottom part of the 250° oven.

Serve with the tartar sauce and creamy coleslaw.

SALMON IN CRANBERRY DIJON SAUCE

As a good Catholic boy brought up in a lower middle-class home in Seattle, I had salmon a lot. It was inexpensive at the time so it was served at least once a week. Needless to say, I'm tired of it, but my family loves it. So this is a delicious compromise I can live with.

The Salmon
3 pounds salmon fillet
½ cup butter (1 stick)
2-3 lemons
1 tablespoon dill, dried or fresh
Salt to taste
Pepper to taste

Preheat oven to 350°.

Place salmon fillets skin side down in a glass baking dish big enough so the fish doesn't overlap. Salt and pepper the meat. Thinly slice butter and lemons and place them on top of the salmon, covering most of the meat. Sprinkle dill on top.

Bake the salmon for 25-30 minutes.

The Sauce
1 tablespoon olive oil
2 tablespoons chopped shallots
4 tablespoons Dijon mustard
3 tablespoons red wine vinegar
1 16-ounce can whole cranberry relish or chutney
Salt
Pepper

In a small saucepan, heat the oil and sauté the chopped shallots until tender, about 3 minutes. Add the mustard, vinegar, and cranberries. Heat to boiling and reduce to a simmer for about 12-15 minutes. Add salt and pepper to taste.

The Finale
Place one salmon steak on a plate and ladle sauce over and serve.

Accompany with Caesar Coleslaw (page 89) and saffron rice.

HALIBUT WITH TOMATO-SPINACH SAUCE

This is one of my youngest son's favorite dishes. Serve this with one of my garlic mashed potato recipes (pages 118-119).

The Halibut
4 pounds halibut
Salt
Pepper
½ cup unsalted butter (1 stick)
3 lemons
1 cup white wine
3 chayote squash

Place the halibut in a glass baking dish and sprinkle with salt and pepper. Cut the butter into ½-inch chunks and place on top of the fish. Slice the lemons and also place on top of the fish. Peel and core the chayote squash and cut into 1-inch chunks. Add to the baking dish beside the halibut.

Cover the fish and bake in a 350° oven for 20-40 minutes, depending on the thickness. Always check the fish after 20 minutes by taking a fork and gently separating the fish in the middle. It should have a uniform white color. This way you will never have dry fish.

The Sauce
½ cup chopped shallots
½ cup white wine vinegar
½ cup white wine
1 cup heavy cream
1 cup unsalted butter, chilled (2 sticks)
3 medium tomatoes, seeded and chopped
1 cup spinach, packed

Combine the shallots and vinegar in a saucepan and boil until most of the liquid has evaporated, 4-5 minutes. Add wine and boil until it has almost evaporated. Whisk in cream, remove from heat, and set aside.

Just before serving heat the sauce and whisk in the butter, 1 tablespoon at a time, until it is all melted. Add the tomatoes and spinach and simmer 3 minutes until the spinach is properly wilted.

Spoon some mashed potatoes in the middle of the plate. Top with a piece of halibut. Put a helping of squash around the potatoes. Spoon the sauce over the top and enjoy!

Salads

CAESAR COLESLAW

The Dressing

4 garlic cloves, chopped
Juice of 1 lemon
1 ½ tablespoons Worcestershire sauce
4 tablespoons red wine vinegar
2 tablespoons Dijon mustard
1 egg, raw or coddled
1 ounce canned anchovies
1 cup olive oil
Pepper to taste

Blend all but oil in a food processor and slowly pour the olive oil in as the machine is running. Add freshly ground pepper.

Note: To coddle an egg bring a saucepan of enough water to cover the egg to a boil. Carefully place the egg in the boiling water for 20 seconds. This should kill any threat of salmonella.

The Main Event

1 head green cabbage, shredded
½ head purple cabbage, shredded
2 large carrots, grated
8 green onions, chopped

Combine all four ingredients in a large bowl. Toss with the dressing.

CAESAR SALAD

This salad dressing is so good you will never order it in a restaurant again. I like to say my Caesar dressing is like my personality, just slightly offensive.

Basic Caesar Dressing

4 garlic cloves, chopped
Juice of 1 lemon
1 ½ tablespoons Worcestershire sauce
3 tablespoons red wine vinegar
2 tablespoons Dijon mustard
1 egg, raw or coddled
1 ounce canned anchovies
1 cup extra virgin olive oil
Pepper to taste

Blend first seven ingredients in a food processor and slowly pour the olive oil in as the machine is running. Add fresh ground pepper and serve.

Note: To coddle an egg, bring a saucepan of enough water to cover the egg to a boil. Carefully place the egg in the boiling water for 20 seconds. This should kill any threat of salmonella.

Creamy Caesar Dressing

6-8 garlic cloves, chopped
6 anchovies, chopped
1 cup mayonnaise
½ cup buttermilk
Juice of ½ lemon
2-3 dashes Worcestershire sauce

Blend together all ingredients.

The Caesar Salad

2 bunches romaine lettuce
1 cup freshly grated Parmesan cheese
Croutons (optional)

Tear the lettuce into bite-size pieces and combine with the Parmesan cheese and croutons. Add the dressing of your choice—basic or creamy.

BROCCOLI SALAD

1 cup mayonnaise
¼ cup red wine vinegar
¾ cup granulated sugar
Broccoli crowns (amount depends on how much salad you want to make)
1/2 cup sunflower kernels, salted
Red onion (½ for small salad, 1 full for large salad)**, chopped**
Red grapes (left whole)
1 pound bacon, cooked crispy and crumbled

Whisk mayonnaise, vinegar, and sugar together in a large bowl. Mix all other ingredients into the bowl with the dressing.

POTATO SALAD

Potato salad is like religion; everybody has an opinion about it. My opinion is to keep it simple and not disguise the natural flavor of the potato itself. Make the salad one or two days ahead for better flavor.

6 medium to large russet potatoes
8 eggs
1 long English cucumber
1 Walla Walla Sweet onion, chopped *(If not available, use 12 green onions, chopped)*
2 cups real mayonnaise
6 tablespoons Durkees
Salt to taste
Pepper to taste

Preheat the oven to 350°.

Wash and pierce the potatoes. Bake for about 45 minutes to an hour. Be careful not to overcook or undercook the potatoes. Check every 10 minutes after the first 45. Remove and cool completely. After cooling the potatoes, peel and chop into bite-size pieces and place in a large bowl.

Place the eggs in a saucepan and cover with water. Bring to a boil and reduce the heat to a simmer for 15 to 20 minutes. Remove from heat and add cold water to cool the eggs. Peel and chop the eggs and add to the potatoes.

Peel the cucumber and cut it in half lengthwise and remove the seeds with a spoon. Then cut it lengthwise 4-5 times more and chop into small pieces. Add to the potatoes with the chopped onion and salt and pepper to taste.

Mix the mayonnaise and Durkees in a separate bowl and fold into the salad. Refrigerate at least 2 hours or overnight.

Durkees can be found in most grocery stores near the mayonnaise and salad dressings.

QUINOA SALAD

This was given to me from Judy Gratten, who happens to be a very good real estate agent and not a bad cook either. Quinoa (KEEN-wa) can be found next to the couscous and risotto section of many grocery stores.

Chipotle Dressing

½ cup olive oil
¼ cup lime juice
1 tablespoon soy sauce
1 canned smoked chipotle pepper
2 teaspoons sugar
2 garlic cloves, minced
1 teaspoon kosher salt
1/3 cup chopped cilantro

Place all the ingredients in a food processor and blend until smooth.

The Salad

½ cup pecans
1 box Inca Red Quinoa
8 green onions, sliced
1 package crumbled feta

In a medium saucepan, add the pecans and roast on medium to medium-high heat until toasted and fragrant, stirring often. Remove from heat and roughly chop.

Cook the quinoa according to the box directions, 2 parts water to 1 part quinoa. Drain and let cool.

Combine the quinoa, onions, pecans, feta, and chipotle dressing in a large bowl and serve at room temperature.

BLUEBERRY WATERMELON
SALAD

Blueberries
Cubed or small balls of watermelon
Sliced fresh basil leaves
Lemon juice

I have omitted the quantities because they can vary. Just mix equal amounts of blueberries and watermelon in a bowl. Thinly slice enough basil to make sure you get a little with each bite. Depending on the size of the salad, I drizzle the juice from ½ to 1 lemon.

PASTA SHRIMP SALAD

This was my mother's favorite summer salad ... I miss her.

1 pound pasta *(Try to find the smallest pasta possible, like stars.)*
4-5 celery stalks
8-10 green onions
1 pound cooked mini shrimp
2 cups frozen peas, thawed
3 cups real mayonnaise

Cook the pasta according to the directions; strain and completely cool. Mince the celery by cutting lengthwise several times and then chopping as small as possible. Chop the onion. Combine all the ingredients in a large bowl and refrigerate overnight.

DEBBIE'S CHINESE SALAD

Debbie has been bringing this salad to an annual potluck for twenty years, and after years of begging, I finally got the recipe out of her.

1 head iceberg or romaine lettuce, torn into bite-size
  pieces
1 bunch green onion, chopped
½ cup almonds, toasted
¼ cup sesame seeds, toasted
1 package Maifun noodles, cooked *(follow directions on*
  package)
½-1 pound shrimp, sautéed in sesame oil
2 teaspoons lemon juice
3 teaspoons rice vinegar
½ teaspoon pepper
1 teaspoon salt
1 teaspoon Accent
2 tablespoons grated ginger
4 tablespoons oil

Combine all ingredients and serve.

TOMATO-BROCCOLI SALAD

This is a simple summertime salad.

4 cups broccoli
1 pint cherry tomatoes
1 tablespoon Dijon mustard
3 tablespoons rice wine vinegar
2 tablespoon fresh oregano, chopped

Steam the broccoli to crisp tender and submerge in ice water to stop the cooking. Drain and place in a large salad bowl and add the next four ingredients. Toss and serve.

CABBAGE SALAD BY WYNONA PHILPOT

Wynona is a neighbor of mine and shared this delicious salad with me. Great summer side dish.

The Dressing

½ cup granulated sugar
½ cup brown cider vinegar
2 tablespoons olive oil
1 teaspoon paprika
1 teaspoon garlic salt
Salt to taste
Pepper to taste

Combine sugar and vinegar and stir until the sugar is dissolved. Add the oil and spices, mix together, and refrigerate.

The Salad

1 medium head of cabbage
1/3 cup finely chopped carrot
½ cup finely chopped celery
1/3 cup finely chopped green pepper
1/3 cup finely chopped red pepper
½ cup finely chopped sweet onion

One hour before serving, combine all the vegetables in a bowl and pour enough of the dressing to coat. Refrigerate.

HEART OF PALM SALAD

8-10 servings

Dressing
½ cup olive oil
1 tablespoon Dijon mustard
Salt to taste
Cracked pepper to taste
1 teaspoon tarragon
1 or more garlic cloves, minced

Combine all but olive oil in small bowl. Whisk in olive oil in a stream.

The Salad
2-3 heads lettuce, preferably red leaf, torn into pieces
4 large tomatoes, cut into wedges
2 cans heart of palm, drained, sliced into rounds *(approx ¼-inch thick)*
Fresh basil leaves, washed and snipped into strips
Approximately ¼ pound Roquefort or other bleu cheese, crumbled
1 cup Kalamata olives, pitted and coarsely chopped *(optional)*

Combine lettuce, tomatoes, hearts of palm, and basil in a large bowl. Toss salad with dressing to taste. Sprinkle with cheese and olives.

TOMATO-AVOCADO SALAD

Best, of course, with tomatoes fresh from the garden but good any time of year.

4 large or 8 medium tomatoes, sliced
1 red onion, thinly sliced
8 ounces fresh mozzarella packed in water, sliced
3 avocados, peeled and sliced
½ cup slivered basil
Extra virgin olive oil

Arrange by alternating the tomatoes, onion, and mozzarella on a plate or platter. Place the avocadoes on top and sprinkle the slivered basil over the salad. Drizzle the olive oil over the salad and serve.

Variation: Drizzle some balsamic vinegar over as well.

Soups

CHESTNUT SOUP

This soup is a Christmas tradition at our house. It takes some time but is well worth it.

5-6 pounds chestnuts in the shell
½ cup unsalted butter (*1 stick*)
2 medium yellow onions, finely chopped
2 teaspoons salt
2 teaspoons white pepper
¼ cup flour
½ gallon whole milk
1 quart heavy cream
1 teaspoon nutmeg
1 cup chopped celery leaves

With a sharp knife, cut an X on the flat side of each chestnut. Bring a pot of water to a boil and simmer the chestnuts in batches of 10-15 at a time for 20 minutes. Peel the chestnuts while they are still warm, taking care to remove the bitter inner skin under the shell. Mash in a bowl or process until they are finely chopped and set aside.

In a large soup pot, melt the butter on medium heat and sauté the onions until they are soft. Add the salt and pepper. Mix in the flour to make a roux and slowly add the milk and cream. Sprinkle in the nutmeg and slowly bring to a simmer. DO NOT BOIL. Stir in the celery leaves and simmer 1 hour, stirring occasionally.

This soup can be made and tastes the best one to two days ahead of your party. After assembly, place in the refrigerator. If it has plastic shelves, place a towel underneath the pot. Also, as with any cream soup, place a towel over the pot under the lid to absorb the condensation that usually forms on the lid.

At time to serve, slowly bring up to heat, stirring occasionally.

ODE TO THE CLAM

By Leslie Fitzpatrick

What is so rare as a clam in June,
then laze in the sun on a warm sand dune?
Say kind sir, can you tell me
where the elusive bivalve may be?
He says, in the sand by the sea,
under those dimples, under big "D"s.
So we get a clam gun
there by the sea,
to get a job done –
a clam under dimple "D".

So down we go diggin' deep,
up to the shoulder makes one weep.
Grabbin' him by the neck
Ain't the way by heck
But a clam is a clam
If you get him out on deck!
Now it's hi-lo and away to the pot
Skilled Digger, or amateur matters not.

For lusciously, scrumptiously,
A razor clam
Is totally, deliciously, the
Best what I am!

JOE'S CLAM CHOWDER

3 pounds razor clams, cleaned
1 pound Fletcher's thick-sliced bacon (regular not peppered or maple)
1-2 yellow onions, chopped
4-5 russet potatoes, peeled and chopped
1 gallon half-and-half

Cut off and discard the neck (tough part) of the razor clams and chop the rest then grind in a food processor.

Chop and fry bacon. Add the onions and sauté until they are opaque. Add the clams, bacon, potatoes, and half-and-half. Simmer until the potatoes are half done. Cool, cover, and put it in the fridge for 2-3 days.

When you're ready to eat, slowly bring to a simmer until the potatoes are to your liking.

To thicken, if desired, wait until the chowder is up to temperature and dissolve 3-4 tablespoons of cornstarch into ¾ cup COLD water. Slowly pour into the chowder while stirring. Repeat if necessary.

Bon Apatite!

NOTE: Razor clams may be dug at Washington's ocean beaches. Occasionally you may purchase them from Central Market, but you usually have to special order.

CHICKEN TORTILLA SOUP

This recipe is for a large crockpot. Halve the ingredients for a smaller crockpot.

2 tablespoons butter
2 cups chopped white onion
2 garlic cloves
2 4-ounce cans green chili peppers
¾ cup cilantro
2 tablespoons crushed oregano
6-8 chicken breasts (halves)
8 ounces Monterey Jack cheese
1 package large flour tortilla shells
Oil for frying tortilla shells.
2 14½-ounce cans diced tomatoes
2 8-ounce cans tomato sauce
About 8 cups chicken broth
3 avocados, diced

Heat the crockpot on high. Add butter. After the butter melts, add onion, garlic, green chili peppers, cilantro, and oregano. Let cook while you do the next steps.

Preheat oven to 350°. Bake chicken for 25 minutes or until done.

While the chicken is baking, grate cheese and put in the fridge. Cut tortillas in 1-inch squares (I use a pizza cutter). Deep fry all the tortilla pieces in a pan with hot oil or a deep fryer until golden brown. You may need to do this in more than one batch. Cover shells and save at room temperture.

Shred cooled chicken into small pieces and add directly to the crockpot along with tomatoes and tomato sauce.

Add chicken broth until the crockpot is full (about 8 cups) and stir up. Cook all day and stir when time allows.

To eat, use a bowl (I get a big one for me) and fill the bottom with the fried tortilla shells. Sprinkle the grated cheese on top and pour on the hot soup. At this point, I add my special hot sauce and avocado. Stir and dinner is served.

ROASTED JALAPEÑO SOUP

2 tablespoons fresh pureed garlic
2 cups chopped onion yellow
2 cups chopped tomatoes
3 ounces fresh jalapeños, well roasted and pureed
2 cups red bell peppers, chopped
4 ounces cilantro, pureed
2 quarts water
¼ cup chicken base (Bases vary in their ingredients; watch the salt—you may need less.)
3 tablespoons butter
3 quarts heavy cream.
Salt
White pepper
1 cup cornstarch.
1 cup cold water

In a stock pot over medium heat, sauté garlic and onions until translucent. Combine all ingredients except salt, pepper, cornstarch, and water. Simmer 20 minutes. Completely dissolve cornstarch in the cold water. Slowly whisk the mixture into the pot until desired thickness. You may not need all of it. Add salt and pepper to taste. Simmer 3 more minutes then remove from heat.

SUNDAY NIGHT FOOTBALL CHILI

Roasting the peppers makes this different from any other chili. The steak makes it more civilized. Barbecuing the steak enhances the flavor.

The Guts

2 pounds sirloin or rib steaks
1 red bell pepper
1 yellow bell pepper
2 Anaheim chilies
1 pound chorizo, chopped
2 tablespoons olive oil
2 medium yellow onions, chopped
8 garlic cloves, chopped
2 jalapeños, chopped
1 tablespoon Worcestershire sauce
1 tablespoon Tabasco sauce or to taste
1 tablespoon dried oregano
2 tablespoons chili powder
1 cups cilantro, chopped
1 tablespoon black pepper
1 teaspoon cayenne pepper
1 28-ounce can tomato sauce
1 28-ounce can chopped tomatoes with juices
2 15 1/3-ounce can dark red kidney beans, drained and rinsed
1 can flat beer

Fire up the barbecue and cook the steaks, 4 minutes per side for medium–rare, and chop into ½-inch pieces.

Blacken the red and yellow peppers and Anaheim chilies and place in a paper bag for 15-20 minutes. Peel, deseed, and chop into ½-inch pieces. Set aside.

Brown the chorizo in a large frying pan. Drain the fat and add to a large pot. Heat the olive oil in the same pan and sauté the onions, garlic, and jalapeños until tender but not brown. Add the chopped roasted peppers and Anaheim chilies, steak, and the remaining ingredients. Simmer for 1 hour.

The Finale
Chopped raw yellow or sweet onion
Shredded sharp Cheddar cheese

Serve in bowls. Top with cheese and onion. Accompany with heated French rolls and green salad.

WASABI WHITE CHILE

This comes from Judy Gratton who adapted it from The Splendid Table's Triple Essence Chicken Soup. The idea is to cook one chicken to make a broth, then use that broth to cook the next chicken. I only cooked two chickens. You could do three if you have the time.

The Chicken Broth

2 4-pound chickens or cut-up chickens *(free-range is best)*
4 quarts water
3 onions, chopped
4 carrots, sliced
3 stalks celery, sliced
4 garlic cloves, chopped

Cook the chicken until ragged. Remove what is left of the chicken, especially the bones. Cool and skim off the fat. Add the next chicken to that broth and cook only until chicken is done. Remove the chicken and cut into bite-size pieces.

The Chile

2 onions, chopped
2 tablespoons chopped garlic
2 tablespoons olive oil
1 quart chicken broth
1 chicken, cooked and cut into bite-size pieces
1 tablespoon ground cumin
Salt to taste
Pepper to taste
2 4-ounce cans chopped green chilies
1 cup green salsa (you choose heat level)
Juice of 1 lime
1 cup chopped cilantro
At least 1 tube of wasabi paste
4-5 tomatillos, peeled and diced
2 large cans small white beans, drained

Sauté the onions and garlic in olive oil until transparent. Add the chicken broth, chicken, cumin, salt, pepper, chilies, salsa, and lime juice. Bring to a boil and simmer down uncovered for about 10 minutes. Add the wasabi and dissolve. Taste for heat. Continue to add wasabi to meet your taste preference. Add the cilantro, tomatillos, and beans and heat through.

The Finale
Limes, cut into wedges
Green onions, chopped
Green olives, pitted and sliced
Sour cream

Place limes, onions, olives, and sour cream in separate bowls. Serve with the chile.

Side Dishes

TOMATO PIE

Great side dish with steak or chicken.

2½ cups Bisquick
2/3 cup milk
3 medium on-the-vine tomatoes
1 sweet onion
1 can heart of palm
½ cup Kalamata olives, sliced
4 tablespoons sliced fresh basil
2 cups sharp Cheddar cheese
1 cup mayonnaise

Preheat oven to 350°.

Mix the Bisquick and milk together in a large bowl. Spray a glass pie pan with vegetable spray and add the biscuit mixture. It will be sticky so spray the palm of your hand and work the mixture around and up the sides using your palm only.

Thinly slice tomatoes, heart of palm, and onions. Layer each vegetable until the pie pan is full.

Mix the cheese and mayonnaise together in a bowl and carefully top the whole pie.

Bake for 40-50 minutes. Serve immediately.

SCALLOPED POTATOES

I have been working on this recipe for years. You can vary the flavor using different cheeses, but this is the best basic scalloped potato dish out there.

4 cups half-and-half (better) or milk
2 packages Knorr hollandaise sauce mix
¼ cup unsalted butter (½ stick)
4 cups sharp Cheddar cheese, shredded
4 large russet potatoes
1 medium yellow onion

The Sauce

Pour the half-and-half into a medium saucepan. Add the 2 packages of hollandaise sauce; mix and whisk until blended. Add butter. Turn the stove on to medium-high and slowly add the cheese 1 cup at a time until completely melted, stirring constantly. The sauce will thicken slightly. When the cheese sauce comes to a slight boil, remove from the heat and start assembling the potatoes and onions.

The Potatoes

Peel and thinly slice the potatoes and onion. In a 15 by 9 by 2-inch glass baking dish, layer enough of the potatoes to cover the bottom. Add 1/3 of the onions on top of the potatoes and pour some of the sauce just to cover. Repeat layering the potatoes and onions, and pour the rest of the sauce in, leaving enough room for the contents to expand without boiling over.

Bake at 350° for 1 hour or until fork tender. If you're in a hurry, you can bake at 400° for 45 minutes, but be careful not to burn. After taking the potatoes out of the oven, let them rest for 10 minutes for a creamer dish. Don't worry—they won't get cold.

Cheesier Scalloped Potatoes

In place of the 4 cups of Cheddar, substitute the following
three cheeses mixed together:

1 1/3 cup Cheddar cheese
1 1/3 cup blue cheese
1 1/3 cup Parmesan cheese

Ham and Scalloped Potatoes
Use a 15 by 10 by 20-inch pan and add slices of ham on top
of the potatoes the last 20 minutes of cooking.

GARLIC AND THYME RED POTATOES

Fairly easy and always good.

1 pound red potatoes, halved or quartered
8 garlic cloves, chopped
6 sprigs of thyme
1 cup Parmesan cheese, grated
2 tablespoons butter
2 tablespoons olive oil

Combine all ingredients in a covered 2-quart casserole dish
and bake in a 350° oven for 1 hour.

MUSHROOM POTATOES

My mother would make these often and add pork chops on the top for the last 30-40 minutes. The added pork flavor made this dish spectacular.

3 large russet potatoes (about 2 pounds), peeled and
  thinly sliced
1 medium yellow onion, chopped
4 cups half-and-half (better) or whole milk
1 package mushroom-onion soup mix
4 cups shredded sharp Cheddar cheese
2 cans cream of mushroom soup

In a large saucepan, whisk the onion soup mix into the half-and-half while still cold. Add the cheese and canned soup. Heat the pan over medium-high heat until the cheese melts completely, stirring often.

In a 15 by 10 by 2-inch glass baking dish, line the bottom with the potatoes, overlapping slightly. Sprinkle with some of the chopped onion. Cover with the mushroom sauce and repeat the layering, sprinkling, and pouring until all is covered.

Cover and bake in a 350° oven for about 1 hour or until the potatoes can be easily pierced with a fork.

SAUSAGE-DIJON POTATOES

3 pounds russet potatoes
8 ounces sweet Italian sausage
1 cup heavy cream
2 tablespoons whole grain Dijon mustard
1 tablespoon regular Dijon mustard
½ cup butter (1 stick)
Salt
Pepper

Peel potatoes, cut into eighths, and boil until fork–tender, about 20-30 minutes.

While the potatoes are boiling, take the sausages, cut the casing lengthwise, and remove. Using a spatula, chop the sausage into hamburger consistency while browning in a frying pan. When browned drain the grease.

When the potatoes are done, drain the water and add the cream, mustard, and butter. Mash until smooth. Mix in the browned sausage. Add salt and pepper to taste.

GARLIC MASHED POTATOES

Garlic potatoes are a favorite of mine. You can make them with roasted garlic as explained below, or just throw in 2-3 cloves per potato in the same water. I can't think of many dishes this would not complement.

Roasted Garlic
2 heads garlic
Olive oil
Salt
Pepper

Bulb side down, take a sharp knife and cut just the tops off the garlic bulb to expose the cloves. Set in the center of a 12 by 12-inch piece of aluminum foil, drizzle with olive oil, salt, and pepper. Wrap the foil, enclosing the garlic completely, and bake in the oven at 350° for 45-60 minutes. Unwrap the bulbs and let cool. Can be made 1 day before use.

Potatoes
4 pounds russet potatoes, peeled and cut into thirds
About 1 tablespoon salt
½ cup butter (1 stick)
1 cup milk or ¾ cup cream
Pepper

Cover potatoes in a pot with cold water and bring to a boil; add 1 tablespoon salt. Boil until a fork easily pierces through the potato. Drain the water and return the potatoes to the pot.

Add the butter and milk. Squeeze the garlic out of the roasted bulbs and mash violently until smooth. Add salt and pepper to taste.

Variations
Add any one of the following to the potatoes after mashing the garlic.
½ pound white Cheddar cheese, grated
½ pound Parmesan cheese, grated
About 4 green onions, chopped
1 cup sour cream

MUSTARD MASHED POTATOES

Careful! These potatoes really have an attitude.

3 pounds russet potatoes
½ cup English dry mustard
1 tablespoon horseradish
½ cup butter (1 stick)
1½ cups buttermilk
1 cup chopped green onion

Pierce the potatoes with a fork and bake in a preheated 400° oven for about 50 minutes. When done, remove from the oven and let cool. Slice the potatoes in half lengthwise and scoop out the pulp with a spoon, place in a saucepan, and discard the skins.

Add the mustard, horseradish, and butter. Mash the potatoes while adding the buttermilk until smooth. Add the green onion. Heat until hot and serve.

TWICE-BAKED POTATO

I'm sure everyone has had a twice-baked potato at one time or another. I'll give you the basic potato recipe, but it can be varied in a number of ways.

Serves 8

Basic Twice-baked Potatoes
4 russet potatoes
1 cup butter *(2 sticks)*
½ cup sour cream
2/3 cup milk
8 green onions, chopped
2 cups Cheddar cheese
½ cup bacon bits

Scrub and rinse the dirt film off the potatoes under warm water. Pierce the potatoes on each side with a fork 3 times per side and bake in a 400° oven for 1 hour. Remove from the oven and let cool about ½ hour.

For each potato, turn it on its side and cut in half lengthwise. Scoop the pulp out into a metal pot or large saucepan with a rounded spoon, careful not to tear the skin. Place the potato shells on a cookie sheet.

Add all of the next ingredients into the pot or saucepan over medium-low heat. Mash well with a potato masher until the butter melts and is well incorporated. Spoon the potato mixture back into the shells. They will be mounded higher than the original shell simply because you have more stuff than before.

Bake in a 350° oven for about 30 minutes until hot and golden. If you want a darker top, place them under the broiler for a few minutes, keeping a watchful eye so they won't burn.

POTATOES
The russet potato is most commonly used, but try baby reds, Yukon golds, or baby whites.

ONIONS
For the green onion, substitute red onion, shallots, chives, sweet onion, or caramelized onions.

CHEESE
Instead of medium Cheddar, try sharp Cheddar, goat cheese, pepper jack cheese, havarti, or Parmesan.

ADDITIONS
Basil, parsley, garlic, roasted garlic, cayenne pepper, jalapeño pepper, roasted red pepper, sun-dried tomatoes, chopped-up heart of palm, artichoke hearts, or broccoli (steam or boil first and finely chop).

Top with sloppy joe mix with jalapeños and cheese (my boy's favorite).

The possibilities are endless.

GARLIC-PARMESAN POTATOES

**3 large russet potatoes, peeled and thinly sliced
(preferably with a mandolin)**
9-10 garlic cloves, chopped
4 tablespoons butter (½ stick)
2 tablespoons canola oil
2 cups shredded Parmesan cheese

Melt the butter and combine with oil, potatoes, and garlic in a large bowl or plastic bag. Mix well. Spread into a 15 by 9 by 2-inch glass baking dish.

Bake in a 400° oven for 45 minutes. Sprinkle the Parmesan cheese on top and bake until golden brown, about 15 minutes.

MUSTARD-LIME POTATOES

**3 pounds baby red potatoes, halved or quartered,
depending on the size**
2 tablespoons butter
2 tablespoons extra virgin olive oil
2 tablespoons Dijon mustard
2 limes, halved

Combine the potatoes, butter, oil, and mustard in a 2-quart baking dish. Cover and bake in a 400° oven for 45-60 minutes until fork tender.

While the potatoes are baking, place the limes on the barbecue grill for about 10 minutes, cut side down. Remove the potatoes from the oven and squeeze the lime juice over and serve.

POTATO PANCAKES

2 pounds russet potatoes, peeled
1 large yellow onion, chopped
2 medium eggs, beaten
4 tablespoons flour
1 tablespoon kosher salt
Ground pepper to taste
½ cup parsley or celery leaves
1 cup vegetable oil

Grate the potatoes and rinse in cold water. Place in a colander to drain and press on top with a towel to remove most of the moisture.

In a large bowl, combine all the ingredients except the oil and mix well. Heat the oil in a large skillet. Take about 1/3 cup of the potato mixture and form a patty in the palm of your hand. Fry about 4 minutes per side until golden brown.

Serve immediately.

JO-JO POTATOES

4 russet potatoes, quartered lengthwise
About ½ cup canola oil

Toss the potatoes in a plastic bag with ½ cup oil. Remove from bag and place on an oiled cookie sheet, cut side down. Bake in a 400° oven for 15 minutes, turn the potatoes to the other side, and bake another 15 minutes. Remove from oven and serve hot.

To add a little flavor to the potatoes, add some spices to the oil in the plastic bag before tossing. Try garlic powder, onion powder, cayenne pepper, or lemon pepper.

DIJON PASTA

I was listening to a couple of chefs on the radio one Saturday afternoon and pasta was the topic. They talked of all the different ways to prepare pasta and sent me into a creative state of mind and this was the result.

1 pound angel hair pasta or any other, if preferred
½ cup olive oil
2 cups chopped tomatoes
6 garlic cloves, minced
½ cup slivered fresh basil
¼ cup Dijon mustard

Cook pasta until the texture is al dente, which means it is tender but still a little firm. Drain the pasta but don't rinse with water. Place in a large bowl. Add the rest of the ingredients. Mix together and serve warm, returning to the stove if necessary.

PESTO

8 garlic cloves
½ cup pine nuts, roasted
1 cup grated Parmesan cheese
1 teaspoon salt
1 teaspoon black pepper
3 cups packed fresh basil leaves
2/3 cup extra virgin olive oil

In your food processor, add the garlic and finely chop. Stop and add the pine nuts, cheese, salt, pepper, and basil. Process until finely chopped. With the motor running, slowly pour the olive oil in a steady stream.

Pesto may be stored covered in the refrigerator up to 1 week.

Not that Ashley is easy, but the potatoes are. She served me these when I visited one warm sunny afternoon. I can't remember what the main course was because I was blown away by the wonderful flavor the potatoes had.

20-ounce package shredded potatoes
16 ounces sour cream
2 cups grated sharp Cheddar cheese
2 tablespoons horseradish
2 tablespoons Dijon mustard
½ medium onion or 8 green onions, chopped
½ cup milk
½ cup Parmesan cheese

Combine the first 7 ingredients in a bowl and transfer to a 2-quart baking dish. Sprinkle the Parmesan cheese on top and bake at 400°, covered for 45 minutes and uncovered for the last 15 to 20 minutes until the Parmesan is golden brown.

This is a very good side dish for just about any Mexican meal. Use the leftover rice for cabbage rolls or meatballs.

8 Anaheim chilies
2 bulbs of garlic
About ½ cup olive oil
Olive oil
Salt
Pepper
2 cups cilantro leaves, chopped
2 cups chicken broth
2 medium yellow onions
2 jalapeños, finely chopped
3 cups long grain white rice

Blacken the Anaheim chilies under the broiler or on the barbecue and place in a sealed paper bag for 20 minutes. Remove from the bag, peel, deseed, and chop the flesh.

Roast the garlic as follows. Bulb side down, take a sharp knife and cut just the tops off the garlic bulb to expose the cloves. Set in the center of a 12 by 12-inch piece of aluminum foil, drizzle with a little olive oil, salt, and pepper. Wrap the foil, enclosing the garlic completely, and bake in the oven at 350° for 45-60 minutes. Unwrap the bulbs and let cool. Can be made 1 day before use.

Squeeze the garlic from their skin and combine with the Anaheim chilies, cilantro, and chicken broth in a food processor. Puree until smooth.

Heat ½ cup olive oil in a heavy pan with a lid. Sauté the onions, jalapeño, and rice until the rice is lightly brown, stirring constantly. Add the pureed garlic mixture, cover, and cook 10-15 minutes over medium-low heat or until rice is tender.

Fluff with a fork and re-cover for about 5 more minutes.

ROASTED PEPPER RICE

This dish goes with fish really well.

1 red pepper
1 yellow pepper
1 orange pepper
4 tablespoons butter (½ stick)
1 cup chopped yellow or sweet onion
4 garlic cloves, chopped
4 cups long grain white rice
8 cups chicken broth.
1 cup chopped green onion
1 cup chopped cilantro

Blacken the peppers on the barbecue or in the oven on broil. Place in a paper bag for 20 minutes. Remove from the bag, peel, and deseed. Chop the peppers and set aside.

Melt the butter in a large pot or pan with a lid. Sauté the onion and garlic on medium-high heat until opaque, about 5 minutes. Add the rice and stir for another 3 minutes. Add the chicken broth, bring to a boil, cover, and reduce heat to low for about 20 minutes or until all the moisture is absorbed.

Remove from the heat and mix in the green onions, cilantro, and chopped peppers. Let stand for 5 minutes and serve.

SAFFRON RICE

This side dish is different and delicious. Saffron is expensive, but a little bit goes a long way.

4 cups chicken broth
¼ teaspoon saffron
2 cups long grain white rice

Put the saffron in the chicken broth and let it sit for 30 minutes. It will turn a beautiful yellow-orange color. In a 3-quart saucepan, combine all ingredients and bring to a boil, stirring once. Cover and simmer 15 minutes. Remove from the heat and let it sit covered another 10-15 minutes. Fluff with a fork and serve.

Variations
Add some chopped green onion or chives.

GREEN BEANS WITH WALNUTS AND ONION

If you're serving this for the holidays, add some slices of red bell pepper as well.

2 teaspoons walnut oil
1 pound fresh green beans
2 tablespoons red onion, chopped
2 tablespoons toasted walnuts
1 teaspoon red wine vinegar
1 teaspoon Dijon mustard
2 tablespoons flat-leaf parsley, chopped

In a sauté pan, add the oil and sauté the beans and onion until the onion is opaque. Add the walnuts, vinegar, and mustard. Sauté another 2 minutes and add the parsley at the end and serve.

Serves 12 *(can easily divide in half)*

5½ cups milk
About 6 tablespoons unsalted butter
½ cup all-purpose flour
2 teaspoons salt
¼ teaspoon freshly grated nutmeg
¼ teaspoon black pepper
4½ cups (18 ounces) grated sharp white Cheddar cheese
2 cups (8 ounces) grated Gruyère or 1½ cups grated
  Palomino Romano cheese
1 pound elbow macaroni
Breadcrumbs

Heat the oven to 375°. Butter a 3-quart casserole dish and set aside.

In medium saucepan set over medium heat, heat the milk.

Melt 6 tablespoons butter in high-sided skillet over medium heat. When butter bubbles, add the flour. Cook, stirring 1 minute. Slowly pour in the hot milk while whisking. Continue cooking, whisking constantly, until the mixture bubbles and becomes thick. Remove the pan from the heat. Stir in the salt, nutmeg, black pepper, 3 cups Cheddar cheese, and 1½ cups Gruyère or 1 cup Palomino Romano. Set cheese sauce aside.

Fill a large saucepan with water. Bring to the boil. Add macaroni and cook 2 to 3 minutes less than directions. Transfer the macaroni to colander, rinse under cold running water, and drain well. Stir macaroni into the reserved cheese sauce.

Pour the mixture into the prepared casserole dish. Sprinkle remaining cheese. Scatter breadcrumbs over the top. Bake until browned on top, about 30 minutes.

BUTTERNUT SQUASH PUREE

2 butternut squash
4 tablespoons butter (½ stick)
Zest of 1 orange
4 tablespoons honey
Salt
Pepper

Halve the squash lengthwise and scoop out the seeds. Place on a baking sheet skin side down and place 2 tablespoons butter in each one. Bake in a 350° oven for 40-60 minutes. Scoop out the flesh and put in a food processor. Add the orange zest, salt and pepper to taste, and honey. Puree until smooth.

TRADITIONAL GARLIC BREAD

½ cup unsalted butter (1 stick)
1 bulb garlic, peeled and chopped (usually around 10 cloves)
1 loaf French bread
¼ cup chopped Italian parsley

In a small saucepan, slowly melt the butter and garlic and simmer for 8-10 minutes. Cut the bread in half lengthwise and spoon the garlic butter over the cut side of the bread, evenly distributing the garlic and butter. Sprinkle with parsley. Close the bread together.

Completely wrap the bread in aluminum foil and bake in a 400° oven for 20-25 minutes.

BAKED BEANS

This recipe complements the true flavor of the bean itself instead of hiding the flavor with sauce.

1 pound dried white navy beans
½ pound bacon, chopped
2 medium ham hocks
Water
1 large yellow onion, chopped
4 garlic cloves, chopped
½ cup maple syrup
2 tablespoons dry English mustard
¾ cup brown sugar
1 cup ketchup
1 tablespoon cider or malt vinegar
Salt

Rinse the beans in cold water and place them in a glass bowl. Put enough cold water to cover beans by 2 inches. Soak for at least 8 hours, preferably overnight.

Get out your slow cooker crockpot. If you don't have a crockpot, then use an ovenproof pot.

Fry the chopped bacon until brown and drain on paper towels.

Put beans and ham hocks in the pot. Add bacon, onion, garlic, maple syrup mustard, sugar, ketchup, and 4½ cups water to the pot and cover. Set the slow cooker to 350° for about 2 hours or until you get a strong simmer. Lower heat to 325° and simmer 4 hours, removing the lid the last 2 hours, stirring occasionally. If using an oven, cover the pot and use the same temperatures and times.

When done stir in cider or malt vinegar. Add salt to taste.

GARLIC BREAD WITH A KICK

Garlic Aioli
1 egg
6-8 Garlic cloves, chopped
3 tablespoons lemon juice
1 tablespoon Dijon mustard
1 teaspoon bottled horseradish
1 cup olive oil

Coddle the egg: Bring a pot of water to a full boil. Slowly lower the egg in the water with a large spoon. Boil for 20 seconds and immediately run under cold water to stop the cooking.

In a processor combine the egg, garlic, lemon juice, Dijon, and horseradish. With the machine running, slowly pour the olive oil until completely incorporated.

The Bread
1 cup garlic aioli
½ cup chopped jarred jalapeños
1 cup thinly sliced hearts of palm
½ cup thinly sliced artichoke hearts
¾ cup shredded Parmesan cheese
¼ cup chopped Italian parsley
2 green onions, chopped
Salt to taste
Pepper to taste
1 large loaf French bread, sliced in half lengthwise

Preheat the oven to 400°.

In a bowl combine all the ingredients except the bread and spread on to the cut side of the French bread. Place the bread on a cookie sheet and bake in the center of the oven until golden and bubbly, about 8-12 minutes. Cool for 5 minutes before slicing.

DILL PICKLES

25 pounds cucumber pickles
1 gallon distilled white vinegar, divided
2 gallons distilled water, divided
3 cups pickling salt, divided
24 teaspoons Fruit Fresh powder
24 teaspoons dill seed
7-8 large bunches dill
5 bags of ice
24 quart mason jars and lids

Place the cucumbers in a sink and fill it with water and about 2-3 bags of ice. Let them soak about 3 hours. Replenish the ice as it melts.

To prepare the brine, combine ½ gallon vinegar, 1 gallon water, and 1½ cups of salt in a large pot and bring to a boil.

In each jar, add 1 teaspoon Fruit Fresh powder, 1 teaspoon dill seed, 3-4 large dill blossoms (1/3 full unpacked), and as many cucumbers as possible. Carefully ladle the hot brine and fill the jar to about ½ inch from the top. Wet the inside of the cap with a clean, damp cloth. Finger tighten the lid, careful not to tighten too much.

Place the jars in a water bath with the water 1-1½ inches over the tops of the lids and boil for about 10 minutes. Remove and let cool. After 12 hours, test the lids by pressing down on the center of the lid. If the lid does not flex up and down the lid is sealed.

Store in a cool dry place for about 6 weeks and then enjoy. If you follow this to the letter, you will never buy store-bought pickles again.

ASPARAGUS

I love fresh asparagus, and it can be prepared in several ways. Boiled, steamed, microwaved with a little water, or—my favorite—baked. Be sure to rinse or soak the asparagus in water before cooking. Pat dry and place on a rimmed baking sheet. Brush about 2-3 tablespoons of olive oil on the asparagus and sprinkle with salt and pepper. Bake in a preheated 375° oven for 15 minutes.

SAFFRON SAUCE FOR ASPARAGUS

½ **cup red wine vinegar**
1 tablespoon honey
1 teaspoon saffron threads
1 cup mayonnaise
2 garlic cloves, minced
½ **cup finely chopped red pepper**

Bring the vinegar, honey, and saffron threads to a boil in a small saucepan on medium-high heat. Remove from the heat and let it cool completely, about 1 hour.

Combine the mayonnaise and garlic in a bowl. Whisk in the saffron mixture. Can be prepared 1 day ahead; cover and refrigerate.

Spoon over cooked asparagus and sprinkle with the chopped red pepper.

ASPARAGUS WITH SHALLOTS AND RED PEPPER

1 pound asparagus
2 large shallots, slivered
3 garlic cloves, chopped
2 tablespoons unsalted butter
2-3 roasted red peppers from a jar, chopped
Olive oil
Salt
Pepper
½ cup Parmesan cheese, grated

Rinse asparagus and pat dry.

Sauté shallots and garlic in butter until just opaque.

Place asparagus on a cookie sheet, drizzle with olive oil, sprinkle the red peppers, shallots, and garlic over the asparagus. Sprinkle with salt and pepper to taste and bake in a 375° oven for 10 minutes. Take the asparagus out and sprinkle with the Parmesan cheese and return to the oven for 5 more minutes. Serve immediately.

Salsas

Salsa's have evolved over the
years and complements just about
any steak, chicken, or fish recipe.

ORANGE AND OLIVE SALSA

Serve on top of any type of fish.

2 11-ounce cans mandarin oranges
½ red onion, thinly sliced
½ cup chopped parsley
15 Kalamata olives, pitted and thinly sliced
2 tablespoons extra virgin olive oil
1 tablespoon grated orange peel
2 tablespoons capers

Toss all ingredients together, season with pepper, and serve at room temperature

CABBAGE SALSA

4 jalapeño chilies, seeded
4 medium tomatoes
½ head green cabbage, thinly sliced like coleslaw
6 garlic cloves, chopped
1 cup chopped cilantro
½ medium red onion, thinly sliced
8 radishes, chopped
2 limes, juiced
1 ounce Tequila

Chop the chilies in a processor and set aside. To seed the tomatoes, cut in half and cut out the whitish part of the main membrane. Take the back of a spoon and pop out the seeds. Chop the tomatoes.

Combine all the ingredients in a salad-type bowl and refrigerate for 1 hour.

JICAMA-KIWI SALSA

3 tablespoons fresh lime juice
1 tablespoon chopped jalapeño chili
1 tablespoon minced ginger
2 teaspoons grated lime peel
3 garlic cloves, chopped
1 cup jicama, cut in match-size pieces
2 cups (about 1 pound) peeled, chopped kiwi
1 cup chopped mango or papaya
1 cup chopped, seeded cucumber
1 cup thinly sliced red onion

Whisk the first 5 ingredients in a bowl to combine. Add the next 5 ingredients and serve with fish, shrimp, scallops, or even barbecued ribs.

AVOCADO SALSA

3-4 medium tomatoes, seeded and chopped
2 large avocadoes, pitted, peeled, and chopped
8 ounces tomatillos, husked, rinsed, and chopped
½ cup chopped red onion
½ cup chopped fresh cilantro
½ red bell pepper, chopped
1 tablespoon chopped garlic
2 tablespoons lime juice
¼ cup olive oil
Salt to taste
Pepper to taste

Gently combine all ingredients and enjoy.

PINEAPPLE-PAPAYA SALSA

2 papayas, peeled and chopped
1 medium pineapple, peeled and chopped
½ red onion, chopped
½ cucumber, peeled and seeded
½ red pepper, chopped
½ cup chopped cilantro
¼ cup chopped basil
4 garlic cloves, chopped
2 limes, chopped
2 tablespoons olive oil
2 jalapeños, chopped (optional)

Combine all ingredients. Keep at room temperature.

Index